The Mosaic Origin of the Pentateuchal Codes

History of the Jewish and Christian Scriptures

By Geerhardus Vos

With and introduction by Professor William Henry Green

PANTIANOS
CLASSICS

Published by Pantianos Classics

ISBN-13: 978-1-78987-512-6

First published in 1886

Contents

Introduction v

Chapter One - Statement and Division of the Subject 8

Chapter Two - History of the Linguistic Argument 10

Chapter Three - The Linguistic Argument Examined 17

Chapter Four - Incompleteness of the Codes 29

Chapter Five - System, Or Disorder? 30

Chapter Six - Contradictions and Repetitions 40

Chapter Seven - Development of Law 43

Chapter Eight - Unity, or Plurality, of Sanctuary? 45

Chapter Nine - The Sacrificial System 50

Chapter Ten - Priests and Levites 54

Chapter Eleven - Levitical and Priestly Revenues 66

Chapter Twelve - Feasts 71

Chapter Thirteen - Unity of Deuteronomy and the Laws of the

Intermediate Books 83

Chapter Fourteen - Internal Evidence for the Mosaic Origin of the Deuteronomic Code.. 91

Chapter Fifteen - Objections Answered 95

Chapter Sixteen - Internal Evidence of the Mosaic Origin of the Laws in Exodus-Numbers... 100

Chapter Seventeen - Testimony of the Historical Books – Judges, First and Second Samuel, First and Second Kings........................ 106

Chapter Eighteen - Testimony of the Early Prophets 112

Chapter Nineteen - Testimony of the Poetical Books 120

Chapter Twenty - Second Kings 22 & Nehemiah 8-10 122

Chapter Twenty-One - Did Moses Write The Laws?..................... 128

Introduction

The author of the following treatise is descended from the French Huguenots. The original name of the family was Vossé, and his ancestors were among the refugees who emigrated to Holland after the revocation of the Edict of Nantes. He received his literary training in the gymnasium at Amsterdam; and after completing his theological course at the Seminary of the Reformed Church of Holland, at Grand Rapids, Mich., of which his father is a professor, he spent two additional years at Princeton Seminary. This treatise was prepared as a thesis in competition for the Hebrew fellowship in the latter institution, which was awarded to him; and he is now pursuing his studies at the University of Berlin.

The subject discussed is the Mosaic origin of the laws of the Pentateuch. This is the point about which the critical battle is raging at present. The literary partition of the Pentateuch, which at one time stood in the forefront of the fray, is now on all hands regarded as a side issue, of whose results the critics of the most recent school of Graf, Kuenen, and Wellhausen still seek to avail themselves, but upon which they do not mainly rest their cause. This part of the question is taken up and disposed of at the outset. The position maintained is perfectly tenable, though it has not heretofore been pressed as it deserves. The divisibility of Genesis, or, as the critics phrase it, the literary analysis of that book, does not in the slightest degree affect the question of the Mosaic authorship of the Pentateuch, or of the laws which the Pentateuch contains. And unless it be pressed to the extent of finding mutually inconsistent narratives in Genesis, and thus impugning the truth of the record and the trustworthiness of the history, the hypothesis is one of purely literary interest, and of no theological consequence. It is only the endeavor to carry the divisive hypothesis through the subsequent books of the Pentateuch, that imperils the ascription of the legislation to Moses, as well as of the volume in which the legislation is found. If Chronicles and Kings could be compiled from antecedent authentic records without prejudice to their canonicity, the same is obviously true of Genesis, the latest limit of whose history is almost three centuries prior to the birth of Moses.

But, if the same analysis is applicable to the books from Exodus onward, the aspect of the case is materially changed. It is indeed conceivable that Moses might have employed different amanuenses to record different classes of laws, and that the literary form of the laws might thus vary to some extent in consequence. But if the later books of the Pentateuch, containing the life and the legislation of Moses, have been compiled from distinct documents in the sense maintained by the advocates of this hypothesis, it is difficult to imagine that Moses could have had any thing to do with the compilation. Accordingly, waiving all discussion as to the applicability of the hypothesis to Genesis, its right is challenged to proceed beyond Exod. 6:3, where God revealed himself to Moses as Jehovah, and this henceforth becomes the predominant name of the Most High; and the barrenness of the unsupported linguistic argument for any division beyond that point is shown.

It would have been better, perhaps, to put the line of demarcation at the opening of the Book of Exodus. For the alternation of divine names is not only of no help to the critics in Exod. 1:1-6:3, but is a source of constant perplexity, which they escape only by conspicuously disregarding it. It did not belong to the subject treated in this volume, to deal with the partition of the historical sections of Exodus. But I think that no one can carefully examine the division of Exod. 1-11, as wrought out by Wellhausen, or by others who attempt a similar nice discrimination, without feeling at every step that the attempt to carry the partition through is a signal failure. The perplexity of the scheme rendered necessary by the rigorous application of critical rules is almost beyond belief. The critical sundering not only rends apart the most intimately connected paragraphs, but throws out isolated clauses and words *ad libitum*, upon the mere *dictum* of the operator, and to save the consistency of the hypothesis. It is simply and evidently a determined forcing through of a foregone conclusion in spite of every consideration that stands in the way.

Pushing the linguistic and literary argument aside, as destitute of any real force in application to this portion of the Pentateuch, the discussion proceeds to grapple with the problems arising out of the constitution and character of the laws themselves, and of the several Codes in which they are found. This is the chosen field of the latest phase of criticism, and it is from this quarter that the materials are drawn for its most formidable assaults upon the authenticity of the Pentateuch and the Mosaic origin of its laws. The issue involved is not merely that of the authorship of a given production, nor whether particular institutions took their rise in one century or in another. It is a question of the veracity of the sacred volume from first to last. The question is fundamentally that between rationalism and supernatural religion. Did the institutions of the Old Testament, and by legitimate and necessary sequence those of the New Testament also, proceed from the revelation of God? or are they the natural outgrowth of the national life of Israel?

The writer of this treatise has decided convictions upon this fundamental matter, and these underlie and shape his whole treatment of the subject. They determine his point of view, but they do not supersede a thorough and candid investigation. On the contrary, they impel to a frank and honest examination of the whole ground of debate: they lead to the patient consideration of every objection that is raised, and every difficulty that is started, in the confident assurance that all the phenomena of the case must find their solution in harmony with what is true and right.

Since the argument is throughout conducted in opposition to the latest critical school, with the purpose of wresting their weapons from their hands, it is necessarily limited to the region within which these critics themselves move, and to considerations whose validity must be conceded even from the stand-point which they occupy. Nothing is gained in controversy with them by adducing testimonies whose genuineness is in question, whose historical character is impugned, or which lie outside of the field which they recognize as the legitimate territory of debate. Hence, no argument is here drawn from the authority of the New Testament, in defense of the Mosaic origin or authorship of the laws of the Pentateuch. And, in the Old Testament, every thing is left out of the account, which, on the critical hypothesis, is judged irrelevant, or which is susceptible of an interpretation consistent with its claims. These may confirm the faith of those who accept the current view of Scripture and of the Mosaic writings, but are not suited to convince or to confute opposers.

It will be found that the discussion contained in this little volume is neither narrow nor superficial. It is the fruit of extensive reading and careful reflection. It is not a summary of results hastily gathered from compendiums at second-hand, but it is drawn from the direct study of original sources. The views of the leading critics are concisely stated on the various points raised in the controversy, substantially as they present them themselves. These are uniformly treated with eminent candor and fairness, while at the same time their weakness and fallacy are skillfully exposed. The book makes no pretensions to be an exhaustive exhibition of the subject. It will not, of course, prove a substitute for more elaborate and extended works; though, to those who are entering upon the study, it will be an admirable introduction to them. And for such as wish to gain a general knowledge of the present state of critical questions concerning the Pentateuch, the range of the discussion, and the arguments employed on each side, I do not know where a more satisfactory exhibition can be found, of what intelligent readers would wish to learn, in so small a compass.

William Henry Green

Princeton, N.J., Jan. 8, 1886

Chapter One - Statement and Division of the Subject

The subject defined by this title is one of very complicated and comprehensive character. Especially since Pentateuch-Criticism has become pre-eminently historical in its most advanced leaders, — the school of Reuss, Kuenen, Wellhausen, and others, — the field of investigation has been so enlarged, and the various arguments have assumed such complex relations to each other, that more space would be required for a full discussion than we can allow ourselves. Pentateuch-Criticism has, to a very large extent, been reduced to a question of facts. A detailed examination of facts must furnish the basis upon which all debate must at present be conducted between the conservative and destructive critics. On account of this comprehensiveness, it will be necessary to define our subject, that every thing which does not properly belong to it, or is not vitally connected with it, may be excluded at the outset.

1. We do not intend to discuss the authenticity of the Pentateuch, but only the Mosaic origin of the Codes which it contains. The latter is independent of the former, though the reverse may not be true. Both questions are connected in so far that the establishment of the Mosaic origin of the Codes would furnish one of the strongest arguments for the authenticity of the whole, since the narrative is in most cases subsidiary to the legislation, and serves as its framework.

2. By the predication of Mosaic origin is not meant that every statute and regulation in particular can be proven to have emanated from the mouth of Moses. From the nature of the case, such proof can never be given. Neither will it be possible to show that the *ipsissima verba* of the law in its present form descend from Moses. All that we intend to make a point of inquiry is, *whether the bulk and essence of the Pentateuchal Codes, in so far as they exhibit the evidences of being one great system of legislation, bear the impress of the Mosaic age*. The origin of each individual part must be estimated by its relation to this systematic whole.

3. The questions whether Moses promulgated the laws that pass under his name, and whether he codified them in written form, should be kept distinct. Abstractly they admit of being separated. How far such separation is supposable in this concrete case will appear hereafter.

4. The problem may be stated in a somewhat different form; viz., whether the law be the immediate product of divine revelation, complete from the first, and not admitting of development, or the final outcome of a long process of growth, oftentimes changed before it petrified into its present form. Is the law soil and seed, or is it the fruit of the religious development of Israel? All these contrasts are nearly synonymous with the great alternative, — Mosaic, or non-Mosaic? The former naturally represents revelation, the latter

8

development. Hence it appears that the unity of the Codes must occupy an important place in the discussion.

5. Our subject is one of wide and important bearings, not only in the department of Criticism, but also of Apologetics. It touches the heart of the Christian conception of revelation. Criticism on the part of our opponents has long since left its independent position, and become subservient to naturalistic tendencies. It manifests a spirit of enmity against the very material upon which it works. The innocent literary aspect of the question has been lost: it is no longer a matter of dilettantism, but of pressing and practical importance, which cannot be confined to the lecture-rooms and studies of the learned, but claims the interest of the Church at large.

We shall endeavor to arrange the numerous questions involved under certain general heads, and choose the following scheme: —

I. Unity of the Pentateuchal Codes.
    A. Unity of the laws in Exodus-Numbers
        1. The linguistic and literary argument.
        2. Incompleteness of the Codes.
        3. System, or disorder?
        4. Contradictions.
        5. Repetitions.
        6. Development of law.
    B. Unity of Deuteronomy and the laws of the intermediate books.
        1. Does a unity of relation exist between Deuteronomy and the Codes of the middle books?
        2. If so, to which of the two must we assign the priority?
II. Internal evidence of the Mosaic origin of the Pentateuchal Codes.
    A. Internal evidence of the Mosaic origin of the Deuteronomic Code.
        1. Direct testimony of the Code to its own origin.
        2. Indirect internal testimony.
        3. The fraud-theory.
    B. Internal evidence of the Mosaic origin of the laws in Exodus-Numbers.
        1. Direct testimony of the laws to their own origin
            a. Simply Mosaic origin claimed.
            b. Codification of laws in written form.
        2. Indirect internal evidence.
III. External evidence of the Mosaic origin of the Pentateuchal Codes.
    A. The testimony of the historical books, Judges, 1 and 2 Samuel 1 and 2 Kings.
    B. Testimony of the early prophets, Hosea, Amos, Isaiah, Micah.
    C. Testimony of the poetical books.
    D. 2 Kings 22 and Nehemiah 8-10.

Chapter Two - History of the Linguistic Argument

The critical examination of the linguistic character of the Pentateuch has been carried on with a double purpose: *a*. To obtain the criteria for an analytical distribution of its contents among the various documents which critics profess to find; *b*. To fix the relative date of these documents. Whilst in the latter respect, however, the linguistic argument is no longer counted as a decisive factor, it has been elaborated for the former purpose to such a degree of minuteness, and with such consummate skill, that at present it constitutes one of the most perplexing phenomena for those who defend the essential unity of the Pentateuch.

For a just estimate of the character and force of the argument, it will be necessary to exhibit not only its historical connection with the discovery of Astruc, but also its logical dependence on the latter. The critics have gradually detached the one from the other, apparently unconscious that in doing so they have destroyed the very basis on which they rest. We must start with a recognition of the very remarkable use of the divine names in Genesis and the first chapters of Exodus. The question, what is the cause of this, cannot be ultimately decided by an interpretation of the much discussed passage, Exod. 6:2,3. If we understand it in the sense that the name Jahveh was previously to this absolutely unknown to the patriarchs and Israelites, it follows immediately that the writer of this passage cannot be the author of the Jehovistic passages which precede, unless we take recourse with Clericus and others to the assumption of a prolepsis, which, however, as Hengstenberg has shown, will not account for the facts. But when we take the passage in its other more probable sense, that God had not previously revealed to Israel those special attributes which constitute him Jahveh, it does not follow immediately, that, by this different interpretation, the interchange of both names is satisfactorily explained. To show that the writer of Exod. 6:2,3, did not absolutely deny the previous knowledge of the name Jahveh, is quite a different thing from explaining how he, acquainted with the facts, could have used both names in the course of the same work in such a peculiar manner.

In favor of the former interpretation, attention has been called to the fact, that, in the Hebrew mind, there was a very intimate connection between the name and the nature of a thing; that the name is never accidental or arbitrary, but the expression of the nature; that consequently not to know God as to his name Jahveh, is equivalent to a not-knowing of his nature as such and the reverse. Nature and name are so indissolubly connected, that, where knowledge of the former is wanting, acquaintance with the latter cannot be imagined. We must admit that there is an amount of truth in this statement: still, it is not sufficient to disprove the possibility of an external proclamation of the divine name previous and preparatory to the actual exhibition of its meaning. Exodus 3:13-15 furnishes a parallel, and shows that nothing else is intended than an announcement of God's purpose to manifest himself in those attributes of his nature emphasized in the name Jahveh, which had already existed, and been used before. As has been remarked, however, this by no means decides the bearing of the passage on the unity of Genesis or the Pentateuch. The point at issue is, whether the various theories which have been proposed by critics in connection with this interpretation can be fairly said to account for the fact, that, in certain portions, Jahveh is used exclusively, in others Elohim, whilst still others are of a mixed character. We must examine the various explanations presented, before we can have any argument, either for unity or diversity of authorship.

The most plausible theory is that of Hengstenberg, Keil, Hävernick, and Kurtz (who afterwards, however, adopted the supplementary hypothesis). They ascribe the alternation of Jahveh and Elohim to intentional adjustment on the part of the writer to the historical circumstances and contents. It is certainly true that both names are not synonymous; but the question remains, whether the difference in their signification accounts for their appearance in all the passages under consideration. It creates a strong presumption against the theory that all these writers, notwithstanding their agreement in principle, still, when they come to apply it in individual cases, differ widely. This shows that their ingenious explanations have not been suggested by the circumstances themselves, but by their own subjective fancy imposed upon them. The very grounds which should have induced the writer to choose one of the names in a certain passage can be shown to have existed for another passage, where the other name is used. Even the principle of Keil, which is that of Hengstenberg in a refined form, does not agree with the facts. The weakness of the whole theory is admitted by a man like Delitzsch. He confesses, that all the ingenuity which Keil has expended on the matter to explain the use of Jahveh or Elohim in each single instance, from their original meaning, might have been applied with the same success had the names been employed in exactly the reverse order. Both Drechsler and Kurtz have retracted their former opinion, which was substantially the same with that of Hengstenberg.

Others have considered the preference of either one of the divine names as due to the peculiarity of the speakers who are introduced by the writer. But this explanation, besides being unsatisfactory in other respects, is only a partial one; as it does not account for the same phenomenon where no persons appear speaking in the narrative.

Some have appealed to mere accident, or to a striving after variety on the part of the author. Delitzsch admits the possibility that the author of Genesis could have used both names alternately, and adduces the Jahveh- and Elohim-Psalms as a parallel. He quotes also Gen. 7:16, 27:27, 28; Exod. 3:4, and other passages. Indeed, if all the passages under consideration were of a similar character, this would be the most easy and simple explanation. But what may be possible abstractly, and even in a few actual cases, becomes highly improbable, nay impossible, when taken as a theory to account for all the phenomena from Gen. 1:1 to Exod. 6:2.

Now, if we could satisfy ourselves with one of these theories, the other evidence which the critics claim to possess of a diversity of authorship would have but little weight. It is of a strictly linguistic character; and how largely the subjective element enters into all such argumentation, needs no special proof. When taken by itself, deprived of the accompanying use of the special divine name, it becomes weak and inconclusive. More than one, to whom the internal literary evidence of analytical criticism has been presented in this light, has been astonished at the credulity of the critics and the extremely fine webs on which their structures are suspended. But here, as in other cases, the evidence is cumulative and mutually sustaining. The strength of their position with regard to the use of the divine names enables the critics seemingly to justify and commend their analytical researches to an extent and with a success which would otherwise have been impossible. Long since, traces of a peculiar *usus loquendi* have been sought, in Elohist sections specially.

We are told, that בְּעֶצֶם הַיּוֹם הַזֶּה, לְמִינוֹ, אֲחֻזָּה, etc., are favorite words and phrases of the Elohist; and they appear wherever the name Elohim appears, as its inseparable satellites. Proceeding on this principle, the critics divide Genesis; and they all agree as to the main results. The bearing of this startling fact upon our question is self-evident. If it can be proved that Genesis consists of at least two documents, and that the writer of each had a plan in mind to continue his narrative until the possession of the Holy Land by the Israelites, the suggestion becomes a natural one to attempt to apply the same tests, so successfully employed in analyzing Genesis, to the subsequent books of the Pentateuch also. And, in fact, the critics claim that they are able to assign each law, or Code, to its original document; and, as far as analysis is concerned, in the main their results agree.

We do not see how the objections to the unity of Genesis on the ground just stated can be answered; neither do we know of any satisfactory answer that has been given as yet. But whilst we cannot enter upon a discussion of this matter, which would open up a field of critical research scarcely less extensive than that of our own subject, we simply wish to indicate how closely the two problems are interwoven. The treatment and solution of the one will necessarily affect that of the other. It is only within the limits to which we are confined that the destructive tendencies of the documentary hypothesis burst upon us in their full light. One might accept it for Genesis, without yielding to the critics in the least with regard to its Mosaic origin. But how can we vindicate this claim if driven to the confession, that the history of the Mosaic age itself has reached us in two distinct documents, bearing the same distinctive marks as in Genesis, and thereby proving themselves to be their continuation? And not to speak of Mosaic origin, how, and to what extent, can we claim unity for a Code that appears to be made up of at least two such documents? It is easy to see how much depends on the answer that we shall give to these and similar questions. If it should become evident that the extreme conservative position with regard to the unity of Genesis has to be abandoned, we can comfort ourselves with the thought that Moses might be, after all, the redactor, and in a modified sense the author, of Genesis. The critical attack does not reach the heart of our camp. It is different here. The vital point around which criticism has moved for several decades in concentric circles, is now made the point of a double attack along the historical and literary lines. Will it prove tenable?

Before we try to answer this question, it may be well to remark, [1] that the history of the linguistic argument is not adapted to inspire confidence in its validity. It was considered form the outset, even by advanced and rationalistic critics, with distrust and reserve. Apart from a few general observations in this line by Spinoza, Simon, and Clericus; apart from Astruc's theory, and the scanty remarks of Eichhorn under the pretentious title, "Proof from the Language," — Ilgen, who first introduced the terms Elohist and Jehovist, was also the first to point out certain peculiarities in style and expressions, and meaning of words; e.g., that the Elohist avoided the use of pronouns, had a tendency towards redundancy, etc. In the main, the argument was either met by direct refutation, or at least by the claim that the materials were not distinct and conspicuous enough to justify the inference of diversity of authorship and of sources. The latter was the prevalent opinion among such men as Hasse, Herbst, Jahn, Sack, and even Ewald. In 1807 De Wette declared that he would not undertake to eliminate the original source from Genesis and the first chapters of Exodus by a purely literary process. The argument found no more favor with Hartmann, who pronounced it perilous and misleading. So largely did this sentiment of aversion and distrust prevail among the critics, that Gesenius, in his "History of the Hebrew Language" (1815), disregarded the claims of Eichhorn and Ilgen entirely. The fragmentary hypothesis was in no wise favorable to the literary criticism. Vater, having established, as he thought, by other than linguistic arguments, the existence of various fragments, expended no labor on that which he esteemed himself fully able to dispense with.

In 1823 the fourth edition of Eichhorn's introduction appeared, and wrought a remarkable change in the indifference with which the argument from language had hitherto been dismissed or ignored. Gramberg worked in the line indicated by Eichhorn, and analyzed Genesis. His methods drew the assent of De Wette, and made even Hartmann less persistent in his opposition; though the latter continued to characterize the linguistic criteria as "indicia fallacia." In the mean while Vater's and Hartmann's criticism had this effect, that it distracted the attention of conservative critics from Genesis, and kept them occupied with the attempt to prove that the laws of Deuteronomy did not essentially differ from those of the preceding books, and that the whole Pentateuch was to be assigned to the Mosaic age. Hengstenberg,

Ranke, and Hävernick, however eminent their achievements on other lines may be, did little thorough and complete work in this direction. Drechsler, though he found much to criticize in the critics from a formal point of view, did not assail their main position. In the main, critics on the conservative side were little concerned about the literary weapons which their opponents were handling with such destructive skill and agility. Herbst thought, in 1841, that he could dismiss the matter without discussion; and Welte, though not wholly omitting it, considered it to be "of very slight importance." On the other side, it was chiefly Stähelin who accomplished the work begun by Eichhorn and others. In 1831, and afterwards in 1844, he gave the linguistic characteristics of Genesis a thorough examination, and turned his attention also to the peculiarities of the Jehovist. To Stähelin's statements, very little that is essential has been added since.

The year 1844 indicated a marked change in the attitude of both parties. Kurtz applied himself to a subtile examination of all that had been claimed in support of the divisive theory, and instituted an accurate and scrutinizing inquiry into the nature and validity of the whole argumentation. His example had this good effect, that henceforth believing critics no longer refrained from meeting their opponents on this field also; though it must be added, that the battle thus auspiciously begun did not issue in their favor. The interest thus awakened, disposed believing scholars to give the matter an unprejudiced and fair consideration; and even Kurtz, who had entered the lists as a defender of the unity of the Pentateuch, was induced by Delitzsch to join the ranks of the Supplementarists. (Second edition of the "History of the Old Covenant," 1858.) But it appeared that Criticism had run, as yet, only half of its course, and could not abide long on the same level with men like Delitzsch and Kurtz. Having gradually won their consent, it now went on to gain new laurels in the construction of ingenious hypotheses. The literary argument had become stale, and could be left with the conservative critics. Hupfeld appeared (1853) with his denial that the Jehovist had supplemented the Elohist; and now not the diversity of both, but their independence of one another, immediately absorbed universal attention. It lay in the nature of the case, that Hupfeld tried to establish his position, not so much by literary criticism as by tracing the nexus of the history. Since the fall of the supplementary hypothesis, and the general acceptance of the documentary hypothesis, the linguistic argument came, if not into disrepute, at least into neglect among the critics. Then the school of Kuenen, Graf, and Wellhausen, with its revival of the historical methods of George, Vatke, and Reuss, took the lead; and, the question having been thus put on a historical basis, the corresponding literary side lost much of the attention it had attracted so largely in former days. Since then, though the critics go on to apply their criteria, and put every line of the Pentateuch to this test, little that is new has been added. Kayser, who has attempted to supply the Graf-Wellhausen theory with a literary basis, uses the argument outside of Genesis only. Kleinert speaks ambiguously of its value. Dillmann has carefully sifted the rich collections of Knobel. Well-hausen finally contents himself with the remark, that it is settled among scholars, that the sections in Genesis which he ascribes to the Jehovist and the second Elohist (JE), are as distinct from the Elohistic portions as they are cognate to each other. Neither, however, is proved, or rests on any more than the gratuitous assumption, that the literary argument has met with unqualified approval in every quarter. With how little right this can be claimed, our short historical sketch has sufficiently shown.

Before turning to the evidence itself, we must make some preliminary remarks, which shall guide us in its examination. They are chiefly the following: —

1. There must be, in the first instance, some reasonable ground why the critical analysis should be applied to the Pentateuchal Code, to justify any use being made of it whatever. If there be no presumptive evidence that it consists of various documents, it will be justly condemned as a most arbitrary and unscientific procedure to divide it into several pieces, more or less strongly marked by linguistic or stylistic peculiarities. The question is not whether the process admits of being made plausible by apparently striking results, but whether it be necessary, or at least natural, on *a priori* considerations. We might take a chapter or poem of any one author, sunder out a page, note the striking expressions, then examine the other parts of the work, combine all the passages where the same terms appear, give them the name of a document, and finally declare that all the rest constitutes a second document, and that the two were interwoven by the hand of a redactor so as to form now an apparent unity. Our first demand, therefore, is that the critical analysis shall rest on a solid foundation, and show its credentials beforehand. So long as this rule is not strictly observed, the analytical methods will be open to the criticism of having created their own criteria; so that it is no wonder, if in the end they seem to be verified by consistent or even plausible results. If we first fabricate our criteria so as to suit the phenomena under consideration, it is no longer a startling fact when these phenomena afterwards appear to fall in with our critical canons.

2. A direct inference from the principle just stated is, that the argument from style and diction has no independent value, unless the differences be so marked, and in such a degree irreconcilable with unity of authorship, that they impress any reader of ordinary discriminating literary taste at first sight. To argue from a few bare phrases and isolated words is simply absurd. The evidence, if it be valid at all, must bear out the literary idiosyncrasy of the author: it must not only be complete and manifold, but constitute one cognate whole. We do not believe that, in the light of this canon, the results of critical analysis will stand very favorably. For centuries and centuries the pretended differences were not discovered, which is a *de facto* proof that they are not of such a nature as may be rightly demanded for independent argumentation.

3. Before a fair conclusion can be reached, we must eliminate the influence which the diversity of subject-matter will always have on both diction and style. Legal language constitutes a genus by itself, and can be judged only by its own characteristics. Furthermore, it is admitted on both sides that the Elohist wrote or copied priestly, ritual law; whilst the Jehovist legislation is chiefly concerned with laying down the fundamental principles of civil life. Now, it is self-evident that the same author, writing on both lines, would be obliged to use a different terminology in each case. The ritual has its own ideas and conceptions, for which certain words are exclusively employed; and so with civil law. The idiom of neither can be expected to re-appear in the other. Only when two laws treat of the same topic, and an actual diversity as defined in the preceding paragraph exists, can we draw a valid inference of diversity of authorship.

4. Due importance must likewise be attached to the context and the situation in which the alleged peculiarities appear. That they recur in certain passages cannot be taken as proof that these together form a separate document. On the contrary, the assertion will stand unproved so long as it is possible that other influences may have caused the appearance of such characteristic expressions in all instances under consideration. We have no right to limit the writers in their selection of phrases, or to confine them to the use of one set of words. Neither can the privilege of employing synonyms be denied them. They may consult their subjective taste, which is always more or less fluctuating, have regard to rhythm in the construction of their sentences, and in many ways be influenced by what they think conducive to fullness and elegance of diction. What the critics must show, is that one class of phenomena testifies to such a developed taste in grammar and style as would render the other class of phenomena insupposable in the same writer. And since it is not possible, in view of our partial acquaintance with the Hebrew, to determine by what considerations the writer may have been led in the use of his vocabulary, or the shaping of his sentences, we must insist upon it, that the critics on their part show the impossibility that such causes should have been at work as might account for the facts consistently with unity of authorship. We must continually remember, that in this whole matter the burden of proof lies on the other side.

5. The critics constantly indulge in certain favorite practices which strongly tend to destroy any thing objective in their argument. One of these is to take a single verse, or half a verse, or even a smaller portion still, out of its natural connection, and attach it to a section from which it is remotely separated, for the simple reason that it does not conform to their literary canons. The method looks very innocent, but it is at bottom extremely deceptive in a twofold aspect: *a.* It begs the question, for thus all traces of an Elohistic *usus loquendi* may be eliminated from Jehovistic sections and the reverse; if this be allowed, the argument might as well be given up. *b.* What the critics in reality do by this method, is just by a dexterous but suspicious movement to

turn in their favor what is in fact against them. That an Elohistic phrase all at once makes its appearance in the midst of a purely Jehovistic environment, is a most perplexing difficulty, which cannot be relieved by declaring it the result of a variety of hands which have been at work upon the composition of the Pentateuch. For it is a sound critical axiom, that diversity of style and diction can only be verified by a comparison of lengthy passages, whose *usus loquendi* is exclusive. Isolated exceptional cases turn back upon the theory, and prove exactly the opposite; viz., that the criteria intermingle, which is tantamount to saying that they are no criteria at all. In every instance in which such a mixture appears, critics must leave it alone; and we have a right to claim it as evidence on our side. Another practice, of which we have a right to complain, is the frequent calling in of a redactor to do away with troublesome facts. When the Sinaitic Decalogue is found to contain certain characteristically Deuteronomic expressions, Wellhausen is ready to assume a Jehovistic redaction to account for it. We need hardly say, that to such cases the same maxim applies which was laid down a moment ago. To us the redactor is as yet no living personality: our belief in his existence will, to a large extent, depend on the estimate we shall put on the critical analysis. It is very obvious, therefore, that to fall back on his mysterious influence for the removal of difficulties, invokes an open *petitio principii*.

[1] The material for this historical sketch has been largely drawn from König: "De criticae sacrae argumento e linguae legibus repetito." (Leipzig, 1879.)

Chapter Three - The Linguistic Argument Examined

When we test the claims of the critics by these principles, the first question is, what *a priori* right have they to analyze the Pentateuchal Codes? The most plausible answer refers us to the use of the divine names in Genesis in connection with the fact, that the writers of the Elohistic and Jehovistic documents had evidently both planned a history covering the time from creation down to the conquest of the Holy Land. Here, however, a difficulty appears. The whole body of Pentateuchal legislation falls after Exod. 6:2, 3; and so the basis on which the right of analysis would rest, breaks down immediately. And, as to the prospective features of the Elohistic and Jehovistic documents, they are most easily accounted for by ascribing them to the redaction of Moses, who may have combined the two so as to form a real unity.

Still, we must admit that these considerations, whilst they deprive the argument of independent value, do not entirely destroy its basis. There can be no objection against here also using the criteria furnished by an analysis of Genesis, where there certainly exists, in the alternation of divine names, an *a priori* right to attempt the analysis. If it were possible to show that they reappear after Exod. 6:2, 3, with the same, or even greater, frequency and regularity, in lengthy coherent passages, which admit of an easy and natural separation from their context, in that case it might not be easy to dispute further the claims of critical analysis to the whole domain of the Pentateuch. Both Kuenen ("Hist. krit. Onderz.," 1861, i. p. 85) and Delitzsch ("Genesis," 4te Ausg., p. 30) put the argument on this basis. As we shall see hereafter, in the hands of less cautious critics it has long since outgrown these modest beginnings.

As far as we have been able to ascertain, the following words and phrases, considered as belonging to the Elohistic *usus loquendi* of Genesis, re-appear after Exod. 6:2, 3. Where they are not too numerous, we shall add the references.

1. מְגֻרִים (*sojournings* or *pilgrimage*), *passim* in Genesis; Exod. vi. 4.

2. אֲחֻזָּה (*possession*), ten times before Exod. vi. 4, *passim* in Leviticus–Numbers, once in an Elohistic passage of Deuteronomy, xxxii. 49.

3. לְדֹרֹתֵיכֶם, לְדֹרֹתָם, לְדֹרֹתָיו, and בְּדֹרֹתָיו (*in his, their,* or *your generations*), four times before Exod. vi. 4, viz., Gen. vi. 9, xvii. 7, 9, 12; *passim* in the middle books.

4. לְמִינוֹ or לְמִינֵהוּ, לְמִינָה, לְמִינֶהֶם (*after his, her,* or *their kind*), sixteen times before Exod. vi. 4, nine times in Leviticus, four times in Deuteronomy.

5. בְּעֶצֶם הַיּוֹם הַזֶּה (*in the self-same day*), three times before Exod. vi. 4, viz., Gen. vii. 13, xvii. 23, 26; three times in Exodus, xii. 17, 41, 51; five times in Leviticus, xxiii. 14 (עַד עֶצֶם), 21, 28, 29, 30; once in an Elohistic passage of Deuteronomy, xxxii. 48.

6. הָקִים בְּרִית (*establish a covenant*), six times before Exod. vi. 4 ; once in Exodus, vi. 4 ; once in Leviticus, xxvi. 9 ; once in Deuteronomy, viii. 18 (נָתַן בְּרִית, Gen. xvii. 2, Num. xxv. 12).

7. בֶּן־נֵכָר (*stranger*), twice before Exod. vi. 4, viz., Gen. xvii. 12, 27 ; once in Exodus, xii. 43 ; once in Leviticus, xxii. 25.

8. נָשִׂיא (*prince*), four times before Exod. vi. 4, viz., Gen. xvii. 20, xxiii. 6, xxv. 16, xxxiv. 2 ; four times in Exodus, xvi. 22, xxii. 28, xxxiv. 31, xxxv. 27 ; once in Leviticus, iv. 22 ; sixty-two times in Numbers.

9. The Hiphil of יָלַד (*beget*), fifty-eight times before Exod. vi. 4 ; once in Leviticus, xxv. 45 ; twice in Numbers, xxvi. 29, 58 ; twice in Deuteronomy, iv. 25, xxviii. 41.

10. מִקְנָה (*bought* or *price*), five times before Exod. vi. 4, viz., Gen. xvii. 12, 13, 23, 27, xxiii. 18 ; once in Exodus, xii. 44 ; four times in Leviticus, xxv. 16, 51, xxvii. 22.

11. עוֹלָם (*for ever*), with a noun in construction, eight times before Exod. vi. 4 ; thirty-eight times in Exodus–Numbers ; four times in Deuteronomy, xiii. 16, xv. 17, xxxiii. 15, 27.

12. כָּל־זָכָר (*every male*), seven times before Exod. vi. 4 ; once in Exodus, xii. 48 ; three times in Leviticus, vi. 18, 29, vii. 6 ; thirteen times in Numbers.

13. שָׁרַץ (*bring forth abundantly*), and שֶׁרֶץ (*creeping thing*), seven times before Exod. vi. 4 ; twice in Exodus, i. 7, viii. 3 ; *passim* in Leviticus ; Deuteronomy xiv. 19.

14. מְאֹד מְאֹד (*exceedingly*), four times before Exod. vi. 4, viz., Gen. vii. 19, xvii. 2, 6, 20 ; once in Exodus, i. 7 ; once in Numbers, xiv. 7.

15. אֶרֶץ כְּנַעַן (*land of Canaan*), *passim* before Exod. vi. 4 ; once in Exodus, xvi. 35 ; three times in Leviticus, xiv. 34, xviii. 3, xxv. 38 ; *passim* in Numbers ; Deuteronomy xxxii. 49.

19

16. פָּרָה וְרָבָה (*be fruitful and multiply*), *passim* in Genesis, Lev. xxvi. 9.

17. מִקְוֵה (*gathering together*), Gen. i. 10, Exod. vii. 19, Lev. xi. 36.

18. אָכְלָה (*food*), four times before Exod. vi. 4, viz., Gen. i. 29, 30, vi. 21, ix. 3 ; once in Exodus, xvi. 15 ; twice in Leviticus, xi. 39, xxv. 6.

19. רָמַשׂ (*creep*), and רֶמֶשׂ (*creeping thing*), *passim* in Genesis ; three times in Leviticus, xi. 44, 46, xx. 25 ; Deuteronomy iv. 18.

20. The emphatic repetition of עָשָׂה with כֵּן (*so he did*), once in Genesis, vi. 22 ; six times in Exodus, vii. 6, xii. 28, 50, xxxix. 32, 43, xl. 16 ; three times in Numbers, i. 54, viii. 20, xvii. 26.

21. The Hiphil of בָּדַל (*separate*), five times in Gen. i. ; once in Exodus, xxvi. 33 ; *passim* in Leviticus ; four times in Deuteronomy, iv. 41, x. 8, xix. 7, xxix. 21.

22. זָכָר וּנְקֵבָה (*male and female*), six times before Exod. vi. 4, viz., Gen. i. 27, v. 2, vi. 19, vii. 3, 9, 16 ; four times in Leviticus, iii. 1, 6 (אִם-אֹ), xii. 7 (אוֹ), xv. 33 (לְ-וְלָ); Deut. iv. 16 (אוֹ).

23. קְהַל עֲדַת-יִשְׂרָאֵל (*the assembly of the congregation of Israel*), Exod. xii. 6, and Num. xiv. 5.

24. לְפִי (*according to*), once before Exod. vi. 4, viz., Gen. xlvii. 12 ; three times in Exodus, xii. 4, xvi. 16, 18 ; twice in Leviticus, xxv. 16, xxvii. 16 ; twice in Numbers, ix. 17, xxvi. 54.

25. נֶפֶשׁ (*soul*), in the sense of "person," *passim* before Exod. vi. 4 ; in Exodus–Numbers, *passim*.

26. גֵּר (*stranger*), twice before Exod. vi. 4, viz., Gen. xv. 13, xxiii. 4 ; Exodus–Deuteronomy, *passim*.

27. תּוֹשָׁב (*sojourner*), once before Exod. vi. 4, viz., Gen. xxiii. 4 ; once in Exodus, xii. 45 ; Lev. xxii. 10 ; seven times in Lev. xxv. ; Num. xxxv. 15.

28. כָּל־בָּשָׂר (*all flesh*), *passim* in Genesis; three times in Leviticus, xvii. 14; Num. xvi. 22, xviii. 15, xxvii. 16; Deut. v. 23.

29. שִׁפְחָה (*maidservant*), *passim* before Exod. vi. 4; Exod. xi. 5, Lev. xix. 20.

30. לְמִשְׁפְּחֹת (*according to families*), with suffixes, *passim* in Genesis; Exodus–Numbers, *passim*.

31. גָּוַע (*expire*), *passim* in Genesis; Num. xvii. 26, 28, xx. 3, 29.

32. שָׁחַט (*slay*), twice before Exod. vi. 4, viz., Gen. xxii. 10, xxxvii. 31; Exodus–Numbers, *passim*.

33. שָׁחַת (*destroy*), in the Piel and Hiphil species, *passim* before Exod. vi. 4; *passim* in Exodus–Deuteronomy.

34. רְכַשׁ (*get*), and רְכוּשׁ (*substance*), *passim* in Genesis; Num. xvi. 32, xxxv. 3.

35. מֵאַת (*hundred*), *passim* in Genesis; *passim* in Exodus–Numbers.

36. שָׁמַע אֶל כ׳ (*hearken unto*), four times before Exod. vi. 4, viz., Gen. iii. 17, xvi. 11, xxi. 17, xxxix. 10; Exod. vi. 9, 16, 20.

37. וְנִכְרְתָה הַנֶּפֶשׁ הַהִוא (*that soul shall be cut off*), Gen. xvii. 14; *passim*, Exodus–Numbers.

38. קִנְיָן (*substance*), Gen. xxxiv. 23, xxxvi. 6; Lev. xxii. 11.

We find accordingly that thirty-eight words and phrases in all, which are claimed in Genesis to belong to the *usus loquendi* of the Elohist, re-appear after Exod. 6:2, 3. At first blush, the not inconsiderable number might impress us; but, after the necessary sifting, a very scanty harvest will remain. There is much in this collection that cannot stand the test of our principles laid down above.

1. Some of these terms occur only in Gen. 17, which is confessedly a chapter of legal contents; so that their re-appearance in the Codes has nothing to do with Elohistic or Jehovistic authorship. The fact, that they are nowhere else found in Genesis, warrants us to consider them as legal expressions. This rules out מִקְנָה [10] (besides Gen. 17, only in 23:18), כָּל־זָכָר [12] (besides Gen. 17, only in 34, and there likewise with reference to circumcision). לְדֹרֹת [7] בֶּן־נֵכָר [3] with suffixes (only once besides Gen. 17, viz., 6:9).

2. Likewise we must exclude from the list all words that occur only once or twice in Genesis, since it is an open fallacy to conclude from such few cases that they are Elohistic. This applies מִקְוֶה[17] (only in Gen. 1:10), the emphatic phrase כֵּן עָשָׂה[20] (once, Gen. 6:22), לְפִי[24] (once in Genesis, 47:12), גֵּר[26] (twice, 15:13, 23:4), תּוֹשָׁב[27] (only in 23:4), שָׁחַט[32] (22:10, 37:31), קִנְיָן[38] (Gen. 34:23, 36:6). In all such cases, the occasional use in Genesis is probably nothing but a prolepsis of legal terms.

3. Neither can we admit as characteristic those words which, though perhaps frequent in Genesis, appear in the Codes in one or two instances at most. It is evident that such isolated words are no index of style. To this class belong מְנָרִים[1] (only in Exod. 6:4), מְאֹד מְאֹד[14] (Exod. 1:7, Num. 14:7), פָּרָה וְרָבָה[16] (Lev. 26:9), שִׁפְחָה[29] (Lev. 19:20), גָּוַע[31] (Num. 17 and 20), רְכֻשׁ[34] and רְכוּשׁ[34] (Num. 16:32, 35:3), שָׁמַע אֶל כ "[36] (only in Exod. 6).

4. Our rule stated above, under No. 5, page 28, forbids us to accept as criteria of the Elohist, words which are found also in confessedly Jehovistic passages. Instances of this are נָשִׂיא[8] (Exod. 22:28 (27)), שָׁחַת[33] (Exod. 21:26, 32:7), שָׁמַע אֶל פ "[36] (Gen. 16:11, Jehovist according to Schrader, Knobel, Kayser, Dillmann; 39:10, Jehovist according to Schrader, Kayser, Dillmann), אֶרֶץ כְּנַעַן[15] (Gen. 47:13, Jehovist according to Schrader, Kayser).

5. Of the residuum, a considerable number of words are so intimately related to the idea to be expressed or the thing to be mentioned, that it is absurd to call in the influence of Elohistic style to explain their occurrence. The thought and expression were inseparable, so that the presence of the former necessarily involved that of the latter. If the Jehovist had found occasion to convey the same ideas, we may expect that he would have employed the same forms. It remains only to ask why these ideas and conceptions are peculiar to the Elohist, but here also the answer is obvious. Critics have assigned the ritual legislation to the Elohist exclusively, and consider his narrative in Genesis as subsidiary to this. It is no wonder, then, that the expressions in question are found neither in the Jehovistic Code nor in the corresponding narrative. We believe that the author did not use them in Exod. 20-23 because he did not touch the subjects which would have given him occasion to do so. The following words are of this character: לְמִינוֹ[4] occurring only where the distinction of species is referred to; and even then it is not used exclusively, for the Elohist knows and employs the synonymous term לְמִשְׁפְּחֹתֵיהֶם also (Gen. 8:19, Elohistic according to Hupfeld, Knobel, Schrader). It is difficult to see how this word could have found a place in the Covenant-law. The only occasions on which the Elohist uses it are in his account of the creation, of the flood, and in the laws of food, Lev. 11. When the Deuteronomist treats of the same topic, he, too, employs the very same expression. עוֹלָם[11] with a noun in construction (often followed by לְדֹרֹתֵיכֶם[3]), and

the phrase וְנִכְרְתָה הַנֶּפֶשׁ הַהִוא appear only as sanctioning laws that constitute the essential peculiarity of the theocratic people, such as circumcision, the passover, offerings, etc., and accordingly could not be looked for in the Covenant-law, which is rather ethical and civil. שָׁרַץ[13] means "to creep;" and, if the Jehovist never employs the word, it is simply because he nowhere refers to a creeping thing. It is so little characteristic of the Elohist, that he himself substitutes for it a number of times the synonym רָמַשׂ[19]. The Hiphil of בָּדַל[21] is evidently a ritual term (compare Ezek. 22:26, 42:20, הִבְדִּיל בֵּין הַקֹּדֶשׁ לְחֹל), denoting the divinely constituted difference between "holy" and "profane." Hence also it occurs in Gen. 1, where the various created bodies and elements are represented as classified and distinguished from the beginning according to a principle that regulated the plan of a holy Creator. Of course, the Jehovistic legislation is not concerned with such distinctions. זָכָר וּנְקֵבָה[22] denotes the physical sex-distinction: to designate the ethical personality, the Elohist chooses אִישׁ וְאִשְׁתּוֹ as well as the Jehovist (Exod. 36:6; Lev. 23:29, 38; Num. 5:6, 6:2. 30:17). And the Jehovist knows זָכָר וּנְקֵבָה also, and uses it occasionally (Gen. 7:3, Jehovist according to Schrader, Knobel). נֶפֶשׁ[25] in the sense of "person:" An examination of the passages in Genesis discloses the fact that the word occurs almost exclusively (when it has this sense of "person") in connection with numerals. This explains fully why it does not re-appear in the Covenant-law, but rather in Leviticus and Numbers. There it denotes frequently the legal personality of man, that which constitutes him responsible to God and his law. Hence the frequent use of נֶפֶשׁ כִּי to introduce certain laws, especially in Leviticus. That this introduction is lacking in Exod. 20-23 is partly accounted for by the general (less personal or individual) tenor of these laws, partly because, as Keil remarks, in many of them the predicate of the sentence makes provision rather for the object than for the subject of the action referred to, so that the construction of the sentence forbade the emphatic, personal mention of the subject by נֶפֶשׁ כִּי at the beginning. מְאַת[35] in construction, is not characteristic of the Elohist; since he uses the absolute state just as frequently, and the Jehovistic legislation had no occasion to employ this numeral. The expressions הֵקִים בְּרִית[6] and נָתַן בְּרִית are not entirely synonymous with the Jehovistic כָּרַת בְּרִית. In the latter, the idea of a covenant made with sacrifice is rendered prominent, and the concurrence of two parties emphasized (compare Ps. 50:6); whilst in הֵקִים בְּרִית and נָתַן בְּרִית, the fact is brought out, that the covenant-relation springs from God's free grace; that he stoops to man, and *establishes* his Covenant amongst men, who could not advance to meet him. It is quite natural, therefore, that in Exod. 20-23, the phrase נָתַן בְּרִית should repeatedly occur (23:32, 24:8; compare also 34:27); since, according to 24:4, 5, the Sinaitic covenant was solemnly contracted with the offering up of sacrifices. אֲחֻזָּה [2] occurs only six times outside of the Pentateuch and Joshua, if we except Ezek. 40-48, where it is in frequent use. Num. 32:22, which Schrader and Kayser assign to the Jehovist, shows that the word does not belong exclusively to the Elohistic diction. It denotes permanent and firmly held property, in contrast with the unsettled, nomadic life of the patriarchs and the Israelites in the desert. This explains its disappearance from the common language after the conquest of Canaan, and its resumption by Ezekiel, who wrote during the captivity. As a proper name, we find it in Gen. 26:26, a passage which Schrader and Kayser give to the Jehovist. בְּעֶצֶם הַיּוֹם הַזֶּה [5] appears twelve times in the Pentateuch; in each of these cases, it serves to mark out the accurate date of a momentous event: Gen. 7:13, Noah's entering the ark; 17:23, 26, the first circumcision; Exod. 12:17, 41, 51, the exodus from Egypt; Lev. 23:14, the second day of Mazzoth; ver. 21, the feast of weeks; ver. 28, 29, 30, the day of atonement; Deut. 32:48, the announcement of Moses' death.

It is an exceedingly small group to which the host of "satellites" marshaled by the critics has thus gradually dwindled clown. Three words only, אֶכְלָה,[18] the Hiphil of יָלַד,[9] and כָּל-בָּשָׂר,[28] have not found an explanation. The last two are found only once in the Levitical code, the first one twice. The Qal-species of ילד, which (in the sense of "begetting") the critics claim as characteristically Jehovistic, does not occur in Exod. 20-23; for in 20:4 it means "to bear." The fact that these three terms occur only in the Levitical law is hardly striking enough to need an explanation.

If thus the argument drawn from the Elohistic *usus loquendi* of Genesis proves to be worthless, we can have no great expectations of the independent evidence collected from the Codes themselves. To say that the Levitical law employs a ceremonial terminology which is wanting in the Jehovistic parts of Exodus, is true, but so much so that it amounts to a truism. What use is there in arraying a list of names of utensils and implements of the tabernacle, parts of the priestly apparel, etc., and then declaring that they belong exclusively to the Elohist? Still, Knobel has taken pains to do this! Again, what can be made of the Jehovist not using a sacrificial phrase like בֵּין הָעַרְבַּיִם (*between the evenings*), or such as refer specifically to the religious life of Israel, on which the Jehovist did not legislate at all? It sounds strange when we hear מִקְרָא קֹדֶשׁ (*holy convocation*) classed as an Elohistic phrase. Do the critics mean, that in the time of Jehoshaphat, or whatever date they may choose to fix for the origin of the Covenant-law, no such "holy convocations" were held? And, if not, where is the slightest trace of proof that the Jehovist has another word to designate the same thing? We cannot but infer that he had no occasion to use the word, and that this is the one and the only reason why the word is not found in his vocabulary. He does use a similar phrase, however, in Exod. 22:30 (31); viz., אַנְשֵׁי קֹדֶשׁ (*holy men*). What is to be thought of Elohistic words which do not occur even once in the whole book of Leviticus, such as צְבָאוֹת (*hosts*), שְׁפָטִים (*judgments*), or of עֲמִית (*neighbor*), which appears only in laws of injury done to a neighbor, whilst, moreover, the Elohist employs the synonymous שָׁכֵן and רֵעַ common with the Jehovist just as well? Besides אֶזְרַח הָאָרֶץ, the Old Testament knows no other word for "native of the land;" and so we will have to hold that its absence in the Jehovist has no further cause than a want of occasion to use it. It is useless to collect here all the pretended evidence of this and like character, except in so far as it might furnish an apt illustration of the ease with which some critics make the transition from proving a theory to applying it, all the while forgetting that their application, as it results in a *reductio ad absurdum*, instead of fortifying, practically weakens, all the previous evidence.

We now turn to the Jehovistic part of the Mosaic Code. The passages, Exod. 12:24-27, 13:3-10, 11-16, are assigned to it by Knobel, Dillmann, Nöldeke, Schrader, Kayser (Dillmann and Kayser, in addition, 12:21-24). Here, also, it is claimed that the dissection rests on solid literary grounds, which we shall have to examine.

First, the proper name מִצְרַיִם (*Egypt*), not preceded by the usual אֶרֶץ (land), 12:27. But neither form, with or without אֶרֶץ is exclusively used by either the Jehovist or the Elohist. The former uses the form with אֶרֶץ, Gen. 13:10 (according to Schrader, Knobel, Kayser, Dillmann), and 21:21 (according to Kayser); also Exod. 22:20. The Elohist, on the other hand, employs that without אֶרֶץ, Gen. 46:6-8 (according to Hupfeld, Knobel, Schrader, Dillmann).

Next comes בֵּית עֲבָדִים (*house of bondmen*), 13:3, 4. This is used only here and in 20:2; also four times in Deuteronomy. But the fact that the phrase does not occur before the exodus shows that its use does not depend on the style of the writer, but on the intention of the law-giver. The reference to the bondage of Egypt is urged as a motive to faithful observance of God's commands; and, of course, this was only appropriate in such laws as directly reminded the people of their sojourn in Egypt (Passover, Mazzoth, Treatment of strangers and servants), and suited ethical commands better than ceremonial prescriptions, which were given to the priests, not addressed to the people in general.

חֹדֶשׁ אָבִיב (*the month Abib*), 13:4; also, 23:15, 34:18; Deut. 16:1. A comparison of all the passages will show, that, wherever a specific date is given, the month is numbered also; and, wherever the date is left indefinite, the month is designated by the name Abib. In all these pretended Jehovistic passages, there is no specification; and accordingly Abib is retained. Of Wellhausen's assertion, that the custom of numbering the months, in connection with the adoption of the spring era, was derived from the Babylonians during the captivity, we shall have occasion to speak hereafter.

נִשְׁבַּע יְהֹוָה (*Jehovah sware*), 13:5, 11, 32:13, 33:1. But the Levitical law contains no reference to God's swearing, neither is it easy to see at what occasion it could have introduced God as doing so.

The enumeration of the seven Canaanitish nations, 13:5; also, 23:23, 28, 33:2, 34:11. But it is not merely this complete enumeration which is peculiar to the Jehovist, but the idea that the Israelites shall possess the land of the Canaanite tribes. He conveys this idea without the same enumeration, Gen. 13:7, 34:30: in Exod. 23:28, only three tribes are mentioned. That the idea is found with him rather than with the Elohist is natural; since the critics assign to the latter only ritual law, with which it stands in no way related. And, even if we suppose that it was peculiar to the Jehovistic document in Genesis, what wonder would there be in Moses' repeating the phrase? How do we know that he cannot have appropriated some elements of the diction of the documents?

אֶרֶץ זָבַת חָלָב וּדְבָשׁ (*land flowing with milk and honey*), 13:5, 33:3. This phrase occurs also in Lev. 20:24. In Num. 14:8, Schrader is obliged to divide a single verse to eliminate it from an Elohistic context. This must accordingly be given up as peculiarly Jehovistic.

גְּבוּל (*quarters or borders*), 13:7, occurs in the Elohistic passages, Gen. 23:12; Num. 20:23, 34:3, 6, 35:26, and elsewhere. How this can be called Jehovistic may remain for the critics to determine. The word occurs throughout the whole Old Testament.

בַּעֲבוּר (*because*), 13:8; also, 19:9, 20:20; *passim* in Genesis. The expression is of frequent occurrence in the Old Testament, from Amos down to Chronicles. It is absurd to call it the peculiar property of the Jehovist, since it belonged evidently to the common stock of the language.

מִחָר (*in time to come*), Exod. 13:14, 32:5; Num. 4:25, 16:7, 16. The two latter passages are both Nöldeke and Schrader assigned to the Elohist, so that the word ceases to be characteristically Jehovistic. Moreover, the Elohist has it in somewhat different form, מִמָּחֳרָת, Lev. 23:11, 15, 16.

With regard to the Decalogue our task is easy; since the critics all admit that the criteria of Jehovist, Elohist, and Deuteronomist intermingle. The sanction added to the Sabbath-command, ver. 11, refers back to the Elohistic account of the creation. Also the phrase עָשָׂה מְלָאכָה (*do work*) is Elohistic. בִּשְׁעָרֶיךָ (*in thy gates*), in ver. 10, is Deuteronomic. Wellhausen claims the same for the whole of ver. 6. מִבֵּית עֲבָדִים (*from the house of bondmen*) is Jehovistic. The whole Decalogue, however, forms a strict unit, and the critical analysis will not apply. To assume a post-Deuteronomic redaction, or even modifications later than the final redaction of the Pentateuch (Dillmann), seems precarious, and in the highest degree improbable. Everybody who has no preconceived idea that the Pentateuch must necessarily be of composite character, and have gone through a series of redactions, will not fail to find in these phenomena a striking proof that the author of the legislation employed words from the Elohistic, Jehovistic, and Deuteronomic vocabulary promiscuously.

The passage, Exod. 20:18-ch. 23, remains to be examined. Here also we have an illustration of criteria intermingling, on account of which the redactor is again resorted to. Wellhausen assigns chap. 21-23 to J. [1] Dillmann thinks they were taken by B (Wellhausen's E) from another source. With regard to 34:10-25, Dillmann tries to vindicate the authorship of C; whilst Wellhausen assumes a *tertium quid,* an unknown source, neither Q nor J nor E, from which this piece alone has been preserved to us. Dillmann, moreover, gives as his opinion that the whole passage, 34:1-28, is out of place in the present connection, and stood in C originally, behind 20:20, 24:1, 2; so that the redactor must have taken the twofold liberty of first substituting the Covenant-laws, 20-23, for those found in C (now chap. 34:10-26), and of afterwards using the opportunity offered him by the breach and restoration of the Covenant, to resume what he had first thrown out. It is alike needless and useless to follow the critics into this labyrinth of dissections, transpositions, and interpolations, by which they condemn themselves, and frequently each other. Perhaps a dozen other ways might be devised to transform a beautifully connected passage into a miserable patchwork. A comparison of the criteria will suffice to convince any unprejudiced mind how impossible it is to prove diversity of authorship on literary grounds. For the traces of B, compare Dillmann, "Exodus," p. 220. To C belong, amongst others, חָצָה (divide), 21:35; צָעַק (cry), 22:22; הַשָּׂדֶה חַיַּת (beast of the field), 23:12; יוּמַת מוֹת (shall surely be put to death), passim; רַק (only), 21:19; קִלֵּל (curse), 21:17. Of A we note the following words: נָשִׂיא (prince, ruler), 22:27; גֵר (stranger), 22:20; שָׁחַת (destroy),21:27; מִצְרַיִם אֶרֶץ (land of Egypt), 21:20, 23:8; אַף חָרָה (anger burn), 22:23 (in Genesis the Jehovist is said to use חָרָה as impersonal, with the preposition לְ).The statement in 23:18 has a Deuteronomic color.

In Leviticus, chap. 17-26 have been partially denied to the Elohist. Ewald, Nöldeke, and Schrader accounted for the peculiarity of chap. 18-20 by the use which the Elohist had made of an older Code. Graf assigned 17-22, 25, 26, to Ezekiel. Kayser, not content to deal with the material in such a summary way, institutes a marvelous analysis carried out with hair-splitting *finesse*. He agrees with Graf in considering Ezekiel as the author, and confidently claimed in 1874 to have settled this fact beyond the possibility of doubt. Three years afterwards, however, this theory had been already superseded; since Klostermann instituted a still closer comparison between Ezekiel and these chapters, which showed, that, with much similarity, there were also considerable differences in expression, making the view untenable. With him Kuenen and Nöldeke agreed; whereupon the former with Wellhausen reversed the order, and declared the chapters one of the earliest exilic bodies of law composed in dependence upon Ezekiel, a sort of bridge between him and the Pentateuchal Codes. Dillmann says emphatically that for all this there is no ground in the contents and language of these chapters, which he regards as containing very old, even some of the oldest, laws. The redactor composed the collection from two different redactions of what Dillmann calls the "Sinaitic Law," these two redactions being respectively those of the Elohist and the Jehovist.

Where there is so much disagreement among the critics, it seems superfluous to discuss the numerous divisions of which the majority must necessarily be wrong. The greater part of the peculiar expressions stated by Kayser (p. 66) arise naturally from the contents: some express ideas that occur only here; several of them are confessedly Jehovistic, others Elohistic; the whole division is arbitrary and precarious, one of the most striking proofs that the critical analysis, if consistently carried out, issues in absurdities. Often a single verse is sundered out, because it presents traces of the Elohist. And after all, Kayser himself is obliged to confess that the elimination of the new source ("law of holiness"), though constituting a connected and somewhat cognate whole, leaves the remaining parts incoherent and detached, without any central idea, or guiding principle of connection.

It may still further be remarked, that the denial of the Elohist origin of Num. 8:23-26 (Kayser assigns it to the redactor) does not rest on literary considerations, but is maintained in direct opposition to the decidedly Elohistic language of these verses, simply on account of a pretended contradiction to chap. 4:30.

We have reached the end of our discussion of the literary argument, and may state as our conclusion that, whatever it be held to prove with regard to Genesis, it is incompetent to prove a diversity of authorship for the Pentateuchal Codes. It appears that the divisive methods partake rather of the nature of an applied hypothesis than of a strictly linguistic argumentation. The conviction that the middle books of the Pentateuch are of a composite character may rest on various grounds. With the newest school it is based on a historical theory of the development of the ceremonial and religious institutions for which of necessity a literary counterpart must be sought. On the whole, the work has been carried out for more than a century with marvelous ingenuity; and the comparatively uniform results need not surprise us. Given the preconceived notion of a composite character in the critic's mind; given the two Codes, though closely related, still sufficiently distinct; given furthermore the acute scrutinizing and analyzing of a century, cautiously fortifying all weak points, and guarding against exposure on any point where any tolerable assertion may avoid it, — and who can wonder, that, under the concurrence of such favorable conditions, results have been obtained that seem to equal in plausibility the skill at work in their production? But the fruit, however beautiful in appearance, has grown on a tree radically different from that rooted in the soil of truly Evangelical Criticism. Let us not appropriate theories and schemes, at the basis of which lie historical conceptions, that we can never make our own. The critics may jump without hesitation from a composite Genesis to a composite legislation: for us there is a wide gulf between the two, and more than Christian prudence prevents us from placing what claims to be one continuous revelation of the living God on our dissecting-tables before we have been furnished with positive and unequivocal proof that it *is* composite. All the evidence hitherto produced is such that it convinces only him who is imbued with the *a priori* belief, that there is no divine revelation in the law: for all others, who repudiate such a belief, it is no more than the outcome of a subtile and ingenious, but none the less unfounded and deceptive, imagination.

[1] In the nomenclature of Wellhausen, the Elohist is Q, the Jehovist JE, made up from two sources, J, the Jahvist, and E, the second Elohist. Dillmann calls the Elohist A, the second Elohist B, and the Jehovist C. This last corresponds, not to the composite Jehovist of Wellhausen, but to what he denominates the Jahvist.

Chapter Four - Incompleteness of the Codes

If we expect in the Mosaic Codes a complete legislation in the modern sense of the word, we shall surely be disappointed. As modern society, or even Roman life, shaped itself, it presents many a feature in its legislation for which the Codes of ancient Israel have no correlative. But the principle of Israel's constitution was radically different. The theocratic idea made every thing subordinate to itself; and the law presents this idea clothed in outward, ceremonial and civil forms. Accordingly, whatever is not so directly related to this one central conception as to be molded and transformed by it, is omitted, and left to existing usage or future provision. In this respect, the law does not preclude development or increase. It has a spirit as well as a letter, however the most recent critics may emphasize the latter, in order to substitute the notion of development for the former. On this point, diametrically opposite objections meet; for, whilst one finds fault with the law on account of incompleteness, another finds it far too elaborate and perfect for a nomad tribe just awaking to the first consciousness of a life of civilization. Both extremes may supplement and correct each other. We should constantly keep in mind, that the Mosaic legislation was intended for a peculiar people, that had a peculiar destiny. It was to live, to a large extent, isolated, and the more it could be protected against contamination by foreign influences, the better. There was no need of a Code that would provide for all the complicated relations that arise from a lively intercourse with surrounding peoples. On the other hand, the agrarian principle, on which the civil law proceeded, secured to every member of the Covenant-people an equal share in the promised inheritance of Canaan. It is obvious how largely this tended to simplify both public and private life among the chosen people. It would be historically wrong to institute a comparison between the Mosaic Codes and the Roman body of law. The Romans were the people of law *par excellence:* in Israel the law was a subordinate means to a higher and spiritual end, subservient and adapted to the peculiar position which the nation occupied, and to its unique calling in the history of God's Church.

Chapter Five - System, Or Disorder?

Another objection frequently raised against the unity of these laws is, that they present all the features of a compiled body, where no guiding-thread combines the collected material. This is indeed doing little honor to the redactor on the part of those who hold the divisive theories. But even among believers in the Mosaic origin and essential unity of the Codes, it is not uncommon to hear the remark made, that they are not arranged systematically on any legal or religious principle, and that the sequence of the laws is only determined by the chronology of their promulgation. This statement, however common it may be, involves a double mistake: First, by laying so much stress on the chronological principle, it tends to awaken the idea that a systematic and a chronological arrangement exclude each other; and secondly, it would seem improper to assert that God, when revealing himself, and his will concerning Israel, in successive acts or stages, should do so without any inherent order.

Chronology is the frame of history; and Israel's history is nothing but the record of God's revelation, its beginning, progress, and fulfillment. Separated from the world, that it might be holy unto God, with Israel every thing becomes subservient to this high calling. Hence its history is not shaped by accident or chance, or according to earthly purposes: it does not run its course independent of God's intentions with regard to his people, but flows from beginning to end in the channels of his revealing grace.

God is a God of order. We must therefore expect, if the law be his revelation, and not the fruit of a blind process of development, to find in it a system, an intended adjustment of part to part, and of each part to the whole, a gradual progress and advance from the more fundamental and simple to the more complex and specified in detail.

This order, if there be any, must be a genetic one. God made Israel his Covenant-people at Sinai. He did not present to them all at once their perfect and complete constitution, requiring immediate conformity to its demands. Gradually and progressively they were organized and built into a theocratic nation, first on a broad basis, then on a more specified plan, till finally the superstructure appeared in its divinely intended perfection and beauty. The process of logic has here become a process in time: the organism is shown to us, not in the reality of completion, but in the mirror of history, only for this very reason the more clear and distinct.

Bertheau has found in the Code of Exodus—Numbers seven groups of Mosaic laws, each of them containing seven series, each series ten commandments. The four hundred and ninety commands thus obtained, according to him, once constituted a Code of purely legal contents, and existed prior to the narrative which now divides the groups, and is often interwoven with them. The hypothesis is very ingenious, but cannot be carried out without great precariousness in details. Reuss has characterized it as "a beautiful illusion."

We shall have occasion to refer to it more than once.

First of all we must consider the charges that have been made against the unity of the feast-laws in Exod. 12 and 13. A survey of the numerous critical divisions proposed cannot be given here. The main divisions, on which all critics more or less agree, have been stated before. They are, Exod. 12: 24-27, 29-39 (except ver. 37), 13:3-16, Jehovistic, the rest Elohistic.

A positive exposition of the essential unity will prove the best argument against all these dissections. (1) 12:1-20 contain the divine institution of Passover and Mazzoth (unleavened bread) *as given to Moses and Aaron*. (2) 12:21-27. The communication of this divine command to the elders of the people, *so far as it was required by immediate necessity*. For the latter reason, only the prescriptions concerning the Passover-lamb are repeated, whilst the announcement of the Mazzoth-law is reserved for a later occasion. Ver. 28 states the fulfilment of this command on the part of the people in the emphatic phrase, "so did they." (3) Ver. 29-42 describe the last plague, the exodus, and how the children of Israel were providentially compelled to leave Egypt with unleavened dough. Ver. 40, *seqq.*, contain a retrospective glance at the whole sojourn in Egypt during four hundred and thirty years, which serves to enforce anew the sacredness of the feast instituted as a memorial of this exodus. (4) Since ver. 38 had stated that a mixed multitude went up with the Israelites, a new provision was made necessary for observance of the feast by strangers. This is given in ver. 43-51. (5) The divine command *to Moses* that the first-born henceforth shall belong to Jehovah, 13:1, 2. (6) The communication of this to the people, ver. 11-16, after Moses had first discharged the second half of the commission received before the exodus, 12:1-20, which was then only partially given to the people on account of the peculiar circumstances, ver. 3-10.

All this forms a well-connected complete narrative; and, as we shall see, it is only a persistent refusal to consider each single part in the light of the whole, that can give some semblance of necessity to the application of the critical knife. A chronological objection has been raised against 12:3; for whilst 11:4 falls evidently on Abib 14, the divine injunction to Moses and Aaron must have been given before the 10th, as on the latter date the lamb was to be selected and set apart. The difficulty disappears on the natural supposition, that the author did not wish to interrupt his narrative of the plagues by this law, and therefore, having reserved it up to this point, uses the account of its execution to mention also its promulgation, though the latter actually took place at least four days before. The expression בַּלַּיְלָה הַזֶּה ver. 8 does not contradict this; for it does not designate the present night, but the night referred to in the context, and spoken of in ver. 6.

Hupfeld's objection, that here a memorial is instituted and observed *ante factum,* has no force at all. The first Passover, as Wellhausen has strikingly remarked, was no memorial feast, it was history; and it was a sacrament, a real instrument of salvation. Of the unwarranted inferences which Wellhausen draws from this, we shall speak hereafter. As to the fact, his statement is correct, and the best answer to Hupfeld's objection.

Kayser alleges that the Elohist alone makes the institution of Pesach (Passover) and Mazzoth precede the facts of which they were memorials, whilst the Jehovist gives the more natural representation that it followed them. This is inaccurate; for the Jehovistic verses, as he reckons them, 12:21-27, treat of the rite, not as to be observed in the remote future, but as in the immediate present, during the night of the exodus: ver. 23 says, "When He seeth the blood upon the lintel," etc.

Common to nearly all the critics is the statement, that the Jehovist (12:34) gives a different explanation of the eating of Mazzoth from the Elohist. The truth is, that neither of them gives an explanation at all. At least, it is not explicitly stated in the narrative. Ver. 34 simply informs us that the Israelites were providentially compelled to take no leaven out of the land of Egypt along on their journey, which certainly had a deeper symbolic meaning; so that it would be exactly the Jehovist, whom the critics charge with having ascribed the origin of such an important usage to so trifling an accident, who intimates the real significance of eating Mazzoth.

But we are told ver. 8 of the Elohist is inconsistent with ver. 34. If the flesh of the Passover-lamb was to be eaten with unleavened bread, and for this purpose, according to ver. 15, all leaven had to be removed, how can it be ascribed to the haste of the Israelites in departing, that they took their dough before it was leavened?

The answer is obvious. According to ver. 21-27, only the first half of God's commission to Moses was communicated to the people before the exodus. Concerning Mazzoth, as yet nothing was said. The Israelites were simply instructed to kill the Passover-lamb, and eat it with unleavened bread. God evidently intended that Moses should confine his immediate instructions to this point. That only the Passover-law was to go into effect before the exodus, is intimated by the peculiar position of ver. 11-14. They apply only to the observance in Egypt; and their insertion between the Pesach-command and the Mazzoth-law shows that the former was, the latter was not, destined for immediate observance in Egypt. Hence the regulations concerning Mazzoth are kept general throughout, as they were evidently adapted to a more remote period in the future. Compare ver. 19 and 20.

Now, if Moses, in agreement with God's purpose, published only the Passover-law immediately; if, further, this law neither commands nor forbids that leaven should be altogether removed, but simply prescribes that the lamb should be eaten *with unleavened bread*, — then it is entirely natural that the Israelites, as yet not knowing that the Passover would be followed by Mazzoth, and that the latter feast would forbid the presence of any leaven in the houses, should have kept their leaven, and were only prevented by their hasty departure in the morning from using it in the preparation of their dough and bread.

But even if we admit that all leaven was actually removed for the observance of this first Passover, still, it is not likely that the Israelites intended to go on their journey without providing leaven. They evidently thought, that, when the Passover-night was past, the prohibition had ceased. God's providence, however, as we have seen, intervened preparatory to the promulgation of the Mazzoth-law. As Ranke has beautifully expressed it, "Jehovah's history and Jehovah's law were made by him the mirror of each other."

Kayser's allegation that ver. 11-13 make a violent separation between 10 and 14, and are accordingly a Jehovistic section interpolated by the redactor, is groundless. The verses are entirely appropriate in this connection when we understand them, as was intimated above. They served, indeed, to make a separation between ver. 10 and 14, though not a violent, but a necessary one, which should indicate that only the Passover-ordinance was to be published immediately before the Exodus.

Neither is it true, as Kayser also asserts, that ver. 22 contradicts ver. 4 and 7. That small households should combine for the purpose of consuming the lamb, does not prove that they joined each other during the night. They could do this the evening before. To press the possessive pronoun in ver. 22, "his house," is absurd.

It is claimed by Hupfeld and Dillmann, that ver. 42 stands very abrupt in its present connection. Hupfeld asserts that it formed originally the close of the section, ver. 1-13; whilst he makes ver. 14 prospective, and belonging to the Mazzoth-law. As Bachmann, however, remarks, the transition from the second person in ver. 1-13 to the third in ver. 42 (לְהוֹצִיאָם) would be very strange. For this reason Dillmann helps himself in another way by carrying the verse back to ver. 39, and assigning it to B; though he finds this hard to reconcile with the expression לְדֹרֹתָם (proper to A), so that he must also call in the redactor to account for its insertion. All this trouble is avoided by giving the verse its natural and unforced meaning. In connection with the retrospective glance at the whole sojourn in Egypt (ver. 40, 41), it contains a new reminder of the sacredness of the feast instituted in memory of the deliverance from so long a bondage.

Dillmann, moreover, objects against the unity of these chapters, that we have here two laws concerning the consecration of the first-born, two concerning Mazzoth, and three about the Passover, of which the second (12:21, seqq.) differs somewhat from the first. The right view of the relation of these laws to each other has been given already, and no other answer is necessary.

Finally, the remark has been made that Moses, in his instruction to the elders (ver. 21, *seqq.*), makes no mention of unleavened bread at all; which would fall in with Kayser's view, who combines these verses with the following Jehovistic section. It is obvious that we have here no *verbatim* report of Moses' words, but simply a summary, which could be all the shorter since the divine injunction had been stated in full. The use of the article in הַפֶּסַח is an independent proof that the *ipsissima verba* of Moses are not retained here.

33

If, then, all the objections urged against the unity of these feast-laws prove irrelevant, we may proceed to the book of the Covenant. The name is derived from Exod. 24:7, and the Mosaic authorship expressly stated in 24:4. Whether it included the Decalogue, it is difficult to determine; but the view that the passage last quoted refers to the Decalogue alone, is certainly untenable. All critics agree that we find in both the oldest preserved Code, though not even this in its original form. Kuenen places its origin in the reign of David, "if not earlier:" still, he has serious objections against the Mosaic authorship. Reuss assigns it to the reign of Jehoshaphat; others, to yet other dates. Proofs in the strictest sense of the word are not given. We simply remark, that whatever arguments are urged in favor of the relative antiquity of this Code, are entirely derived from its peculiar significance and unique place in the constitution of Israel. When Kuenen claims that the laws of Exod. 20-23 distinguish themselves by their simplicity and originality, this is exactly what we would expect of a Code destined to be the fundamental law of Israel, and to present in a few general commands the primary relations and duties devolving upon the Covenant-people. To speak of originality is begging the question, and the simplicity is fully accounted for by the historical situation in which the Pentateuch places it. Indeed, we should be surprised if these commands were less simple, if God had at the outset overwhelmed the Israelites with a mass of ceremonial detail, and on such a basis entered with them into a solemn covenant. Jer. 7:22 gives the right point of view. On the other hand, how natural and fitting is the place of this Code at the beginning of the great career upon which Israel was to enter. The whole is an application of the Decalogue to the most general features of national life. Consequently, in chap. 21:1 we meet the word מִשְׁפָּטִים, designating "the rights by which the national life was formed into a civil commonwealth and the political order secured." Intimately connected with the Decalogue, they start with emphasizing the same principle,—viz., the unity and spirituality of God,—and cover nearly the same ground. Exception has been taken to the lack of the religious element; but the objection leaves out of view Exod. 20:22-26 and 23:14-19, which certainly formed a part of the book of the Covenant.

Next come the directions concerning the building of the sanctuary (chap. 25-30). After the people, by their adhesion to the Covenant, had been constituted the peculiar property of God, their Theocratic King, provisions are made for his dwelling amongst them. The relation having been defined, the first step is taken to realize it in the accurate description of the tabernacle, which would be its symbol and pledge. As Keil expresses it, "A definite external form must be given to the covenant just concluded, a visible bond of fellowship constructed." This is explicitly stated in chap. 25:8, with a clear allusion to 23:20, 21. The critics, otherwise so acute in discovering traces of affinity, where details are concerned seem to be blind for this most intimate relation, which makes one passage grow out of the other in the most natural way. Their dissecting methods seem to have disqualified them for a true appreciation of the theocratic idea, which germinates in the soil of God's Covenant, and thence develops itself into the manifold forms of a system in which the social and religious life interpenetrate.

At first sight the section, chap. 31:12-17, might appear superfluous and out of place. Keil justifies its occurrence by suggesting that the Israelites might have thought it unnecessary or non-obligatory to observe the Sabbath-commandment during the execution of so great a work in honor of Jehovah. With him agree Knobel and Graf. There is nothing in the context, however, to favor this view; and it seems better to explain the emphatic repetition of this law from the great importance of the Sabbath as a Covenant sign between Israel and the Lord. In ver. 13 it is called אוֹת, in ver. 16 בְּרִית. For this reason it is subjoined to that other visible bond of fellowship, the tabernacle. As in the latter, God by his glorious presence signified his gracious attitude towards Israel, so Israel by the observance of this day of rest would show its faithful adherence to Jehovah's Covenant.

We pass on to chap. 34:10-27. As we have seen already, Dillmann recognizes in these verses the Covenant-law of C as it once stood after 20:20 and 24:1, 2, whilst Wellhausen postulates a new source for this passage alone. The fact is, that we have here nothing but a shorter re-enactment and re-statement of the Covenant-law, that had been broken by idolatry. As the first solemn conclusion of the Covenant preceded the gift of the first tables, so, after the latter had been broken, the former must be renewed before the new tables of the Decalogue can be handed to Moses. It was a deep insight into the sinful nature of the people and a clear apprehension of the corrupt tendency manifested in this single act of idolatry, that led to emphasizing specially the prohibition of intercourse with the Canaanites. Also the reference to the golden calf in ver. 17, אֱלֹהֵי מַסֵּכָה, is obvious. Both points of contact with the preceding chapters are disregarded by the divisive critics. It is more difficult to see why, from ver. 18 onward, the feast-laws are restated with slight differences in form from Exod. 23. Partly their religious and theocratic importance may have caused their appearance in this connection: partly their place at the end of the Covenant-law (chap. 23) may account for the fact that they, and not other laws, are repeated. As the first covenant began with the Decalogue, engraven in stone, and closed with the feast-laws, so after the breaking, though there be no formal restatement of every particular, still we find the beginning and end of the former law repeated, to indicate that this new covenant rests on essentially the same basis as the old. The repetition is not pleonastic, but of deep significance. Decalogue and feast-laws stand as representatives of all the contents of the Covenant-book.

The promulgation of the Sabbath-commandment in chap. 35:1-3 is parallel to chap. 31:12-17. Moses had been commissioned to remind the Israelites in particular of this Covenant-sign. Having come down, according to chap. 34:29, he immediately executes this commission as soon as the opportunity offers itself. Here also there are regular progress and perfect connection.

Chap. 35-40 correspond to 30-35, and describe the execution of what was commanded there. Of the peculiar position which chap. 30:1-10 (of the altar of incense) occupies, we must speak hereafter.

The Levitical Code, though forming a unit in its own compass, is nevertheless but a single link in the great chain: as we hope to show, it takes up the development of the Theocracy where Exodus left off, and carries it onward.

The sacrificial laws (chap. 1-7) form, as the closing verses show, a coherent group. Their position at this juncture is not only natural, but necessary. The sacrifices in their whole ritual presuppose the completed sanctuary, the erecting of which was recorded in Exod. 40. Moreover, it is stated (Lev. 1:1), that the Lord called unto Moses, and spake unto him, out of the tabernacle of the congregation, in accordance with his promise (Exod. 25:22). A third reason for our statement that this Code occupies a fitting place in the history of revelation, is that it is so general in its character. No specification being made concerning the time for presentation of sacrifices, or the order in which they were to succeed each other, or the number of the animals to be offered at the various occasions, all which was to be regulated afterwards, the Code confines itself to what was its evident purpose; viz., the laying down of the general principles of sacrificial service as a necessary supplement and completion of the tabernacle-worship. The enumeration of all chief topics proves beyond doubt, that we possess the Code in its original, unaltered condition. The last two chapters refer to the priests, and give special instructions concerning their treatment of sacrifices, which accounts for some repetitions of previous statements.

Chap. 8-10 describe the induction of Aaron and his sons into the priestly office. The fulfillment of the command given at the same time with the directions for the building of the tabernacle could not have been placed earlier, because the laws of sacrifices had a bearing upon this act. It could not have occurred later, because the completed regulation of the tabernacle ceremonial required an officiating priesthood, and waited but for their investiture to go into full operation. Thus we find the place of these three chapters again naturally and necessarily determined by what precedes and follows. Their omission would leave a gap, and their insertion at any other juncture would create a disturbance in the systematic order of the whole.

In chap. 11-25 we find the laws concerning uncleanness, purification, and holiness. They add a new feature to the hitherto imperfect scheme of the Theocracy. We saw its constitution in the Covenant-law, its initial realization in the laws of the sanctuary, the sacrifices, and the priesthood: here our attention is called to the fruits of purity and holiness which this organization was intended to produce, both in a ceremonial and moral aspect. Holiness was the ever-recurring condition of God's dwelling amongst them,—the one great demand, which the ritual was both to symbolize and to effect. First it is only ceremonial and outward purity, announcing itself in the discrimination between clean and unclean animals, and in the purification of the body (11-

15); but this in its turn becomes a type of that higher spiritual and moral doing away of sin, whose completion was foreshadowed in the Day of Atonement (16), and directly urged on the people by the moral commands from chap. 17 onward. It is important to notice how at this very juncture, where the critics claim to have discovered the attachment of an earlier Code ("law of holiness") to a later one, there is the most intimate coherence and connection manifested in a gradual advance from the outward to the inward; from the ritual to the moral; from what is demanded of the people, to what is imposed on the priests, to whom the call for holiness came with double force, and in a more special sense (21); from the everyday life, with its distinction in the daily food, to those holy exercises at the sanctuary, which were to be the highest and most adequate expression of an all-pervading sanctity and entire consecration to God (23). How the theocratic principle has shaped these laws, and determined their sequence, is seen in the fact, that holiness, though required in the most simple acts and forms of life, is ultimately referred to as finding its full realization in religious observances, in sacrifices (22), and holy convocations (23), and its most significant representation in the burning lamps and show-bread of the tabernacle (24:1-9).

The unity of chap. 23 has been doubted and denied on various grounds. Chiefly the frequent repetition of titles, ver. 1, 9, 23, 26, 33, has led to the inference, that the chapter presents a compilation of feast-laws, notwithstanding the undeniable fact that they are all ranged under one general principle,—the holding of a מִקְרָא קֹדֶשׁ (*holy convocation*),— and presented in the strictest chronological order. Dillmann thinks that ver. 9-22, 23-32, 33-43, once formed independent regulations concerning the respective feasts of which they treat. George, Hupfeld, and recently Wellhausen, assumed two complete feast-Codes,— one of the Elohist, ver. 1-8, 23-38; and one of another hand, ver. 9-22, 39-43, interwoven by the redactor. Both assertions are equally gratuitous. The two Codes as separated by Wellhausen are not complete; since the one lacks the feast of weeks, the other Mazzoth. And against both views, that of Dillmann as well as Wellhausen's, stand the uniformity of treatment, the similarity throughout in expression, and the retention of the same leading idea in all the parts. The appearance of a second title in ver. 4 is accounted for by the consideration, that here the מוֹעֲדִים, the appointed seasons proper, begin in distinction from the Sabbath. And how the recurring titles can awake suspicion in critics who are accustomed to comment upon the redundancy of the Elohist, we do not understand. By taking ver. 37, 38, not as the close of the whole preceding chapter, but only of ver. 4-36 (of the מוֹעֲדִים proper), the difficulty arising from the words "beside the Sabbaths" is relieved, and at the same time the reference of ver. 4 to the yearly recurring feasts strikingly confirmed. This view also leaves room for the supplementary Succoth-law (ver. 39-43); since, according to it, ver. 37, 38, do not close the whole, but only a subdivision, of the topic. The final close does not follow until ver. 44. The positive explanation of the supplementary character of ver.

39-43 is best given by Bachmann; viz., that the aspect of the observance described in these verses stood in no direct relation to the מִקְרָא קֹדֶשׁ and the sanctuary, and therefore could be better added subsequently than connected with 34-36, since the latter would have destroyed the unity of the chapter, which is up to that point governed by one central idea. Negatively, the view which holds ver. 39-43 to be an addition of the redactor from a different source is untenable, as Dillmann remarks, against Wellhausen and Kayser. For (a) The Elohist must have given fuller directions concerning Succoth, which he had not as yet treated in detail, than those contained in ver. 34-36. (b) Ver. 39-43 is incomplete: it does not even contain the name of the feast referred to, and requires what precedes for its explanation. (c) The language is Elohistic. We may finally remark, that in chap. 23 special attention is paid to the feasts not exhaustively treated before (Pentecost, Succoth), whilst others, for which full provision had been previously made already, are here more summarily dismissed (Passover, Day of Atonement).

The promulgation of the laws concerning murder, damage, and blasphemy (24:10-23) was occasioned by the blasphemy of Shelomith's son.

The heading of chap. 25 indicates that its contents close the main body of Sinaitic legislation, which accordingly ends with the regulations for the Sabbath-year and the year of jubilee. This position is entirely appropriate. By these institutions the existence and continuance of the theocratic community was insured, by securing a permanent validity to its agrarian basis, which depended, of course, on the equal division of property among all its members.

Chap. 26 formally closes the Levitical Code with a prophetic appeal to the people, urging upon them faithful observance of God's law, and threatening a curse against all disobedience, showing, in a warning disclosure of future apostasy, to what dangers the people would be exposed when once in possession of the promised land. There is a manifest similarity in the closing sections of the Covenant-law, the Levitical Code, and the Deuteronomic legislation, which betrays their essential unity. The Covenant-law made last of all provision for the feasts: so does Leviticus. And as the former was sanctioned by special promises in accordance with its special scope and character (Exod. 23:20-33), so the more voluminous law of Leviticus has its more comprehensive statement of the blessing and curse at its close. Such underlying harmonious unity far outweighs the numerous external contradictions which the critics claim to have discovered in detail. Unity lies at the bottom: the discord is superficial and imaginary.

Chap. 27 treats of vows. Probably the non-obligatory character of this religious service caused its treatment outside of the main body of laws.

During the promulgation of the Levitical Code, the history of the Covenant-people had offered nothing remarkable, which could have been the occasion of the enactment of a new law. With a few exceptions in chap. 8, 9, 10, Leviticus contains no narrative.

In Numbers the historical principle becomes again predominant, as it was in Exodus. There is this difference, however,— that in Exodus the majority of the laws were so important that they influenced history, and drew it into their own appointed course, so that it became subordinate to legislation. In Numbers, on the contrary, much refers to the temporary circumstances of the desert journey, and therefore appears as the historical occasions offered themselves. Accordingly, the systematic arrangement has more and more to give place to an external attachment of legal fragments to the facts of history.

Still, even where the outward unity and connection are wanting, there is a ruling idea, which, as it has determined the history of this period, also has given a common character to its laws. They all relate in some way to the civil and political constitution of Israel, to the external and internal organization of the tribes as the army and the congregation of Jehovah, either as this was determined for the present by the journey towards Canaan (chap. 1-10:10), or required for the future by possession of the Holy Land (22-36). The former of these sections is chiefly legal, the latter of a mixed character: all that falls between them gives the history of the journey from Sinai to the Jordan, interrupted by legal sections in chap. 15, 17, 18, 19.

Bertheau, up to this point having been able to trace a combination of the significant numbers 7 and 10 in various groups and series and decalogues, is now obliged to confess, that only a certain arrangement on the principle of decades can be discovered here.

The remarks made above concerning the chronological position of the laws which occur here, show that a positive vindication of their systematic unity would be in vain. We may content ourselves with answering a few objections raised against the good order of these legal passages.

Bertheau considers Num. 3:1-4 as an insertion, lacking all connection both with what precedes and with what follows, loosely suspended between 2 and 3.

The reason, however, why the generations of Aaron should be given at this juncture, is obvious; viz., to distinguish the priests at the outset from the Levites. Had the service of the latter been described without this distinction being made, it would have appeared as if they stood on a par with the priests. Ver. 6 states emphatically that the Levites were to minister unto *Aaron the priest.*

The first part of chap. 9 has suggested to many a twofold difficulty. (*a*) It seems unnecessary that the Passover-law should have been repeated here without any additional or supplementary directions (ver. 1-5). (*b*) The date mentioned in ver. 1 carries us back before the date given in chap. 1:1.Both difficulties are best removed by considering ver. 1-5 as an introduction to the law of the second Passover, from ver. 6 onward. This instruction was, according to the context, revealed by God to Moses in the first month; i.e., at the regular Passover-time. But the supplementary provision for defiled persons was not made until some time after the regular observance, — according to

1:1, at least fourteen days later. Thus the chapter fits well in the chronology of the book, and ver. 1 repeats a command given a few weeks before to introduce the new provision stated in ver. 6, *seqq.*

Dr. Kuenen objects to chap. 15, that it is evidently an interpolation. His reasons are, that it is not connected with what precedes and follows, and that ver. 2, as it stands now, comes in very inappropriately, and sounds almost like sarcastic irony in the mouth of God, after the events narrated in the two preceding chapters. The fact is, that these laws were given during the thirty-nine years' wandering in the desert. As there is a break in the history here, neither the exact chronological position, nor the historical occasion of the announcement of them, can be determined. The irony would certainly disappear, if, between the judgment of chap. 14 and the directions of chap. 15, some months, or even years, had intervened. Instead of sarcasm and irony, it would seem that there fell a ray of hope and divine consolation on the background of these verses, in so far as the possession of Canaan is alluded to. Probably this was done to remind the rising generation that to them God would keep his promise, and bestow upon them these benefits which their fathers had forfeited by their rebellion and unbelief.

This part, also, of our task is now accomplished. Having shown that all the laws in Exodus - Numbers, so far as language and context are concerned, form one systematic, progressive, well-connected whole, we possess a vantage-ground on which to meet the critics in their next attack upon the unity of the pre-Deuteronomic Codes.

Chapter Six - Contradictions and Repetitions

It is claimed that the Pentateuchal Codes, even when Deuteronomy is left out of view, confront us with cases of flat and irreconcilable contradiction. Of course, if this be true, it precludes most positively all unity of authorship. Two contradictory laws cannot have been in operation at the same time: the one must have been antiquated when the other went into effect. And least of all is it thinkable, the critics say, that the same legislator should have prescribed two contradictory laws, and thus destroyed his own work and authority.

1. It must be admitted, if a number of contradictory laws, exclusive of each other, can be pointed out, without any reason to account for their difference in the altered circumstances, or any explicit statement that the one has been substituted for the other, that in this case we shall be shut up to the denial of the unity, and consequently the Mosaic authorship, of the Code. On the other hand, nothing less than this can accomplish the result, which the critics wish to produce, of putting Moses at variance with himself. A second condition to which this argument is tied, should be that a considerable number of discrepancies be adduced. To argue from a few isolated cases, and to leave the

perfect agreement on the whole out of sight, is to substitute the letter for the spirit, and awakens a strong suspicion against the critics, that they are intent upon making out a case; that it is not the contradictions which compel them to deny the unity, but that *they* strain and press the former unduly to summon them as witnesses against it. It requires a very strong combination of individual facts to overthrow the presumptive evidence in favor of unity, which we have discovered in the remarkable similarity and agreement of all the Codes.

2. Abstractly, all admit the possibility that two laws might apparently contradict each other, whilst the difference might simply arise from the peculiar aim of each. In modern law, instances of such a character are numerous; but, whilst they are abstractly obliged to make this concession, the critics never endeavor to harmonize in concrete cases. This clearly proves that the question at issue is begged from the outset: it is a settled affair with the critics that the Codes are distinct. Thus prejudice and bias deal with the law in an unlawful way, and deprive it of its inherent right to speak for itself. The lawgiver is stopped in the midst of his instructions; and the dislocated and detached sentences of laws thus rendered incomplete, are triumphantly held up as contradicting each other. All such methods must be met with a bold protest; and no reasoning which in its premises anticipates an element of the conclusion to be reached, can be considered as valid.

3. Dr. Kuenen distinguishes two sorts of contradictions: 1. The discrepancy, though it actually exists, is of such a character that exegetical ingenuity, combined with the arts of jurisprudence, can solve the harmonistic problem. 2. The one law positively excludes the other. We must protest against this *a priori* decision of how much jurisprudence may be admitted in the exposition of law. If historical interpretation may be guided by historical canons, why not facilitate the explanation of law by all legal means? That the solution of a complicated legal problem can be reached only with the help of fine distinctions, gives Dr. Kuenen no right to affirm that the discrepancies actually existed in the mind of the lawgiver.

4. If it be admitted that law may and must be interpreted and harmonized on legal principles, we find that there are in general two ways in which apparent contradictions can be removed; and it is but fair to try either of them before an absolute disagreement is alleged.

(*a*) *Systematically* we harmonize two statements by assigning to each its proper domain, considering them from the peculiar point of view which the lawgiver had in mind when he prescribed them, by making the one supplement the other.

(*b*) *Historically* the chronologically later passage must be given the preference over the one enacted earlier. There is nothing unreasonable in the assumption that provisional directions were subsequently modified, especially when at first only stated in outline rather for theoretical than practical purposes. This right of historical harmonization must be insisted on the more firmly, since the Pentateuch presents codified law in the framework of history, from a historical point of view. In many cases, the earlier enactment was not given for a legal, but simply for a historical, purpose, or only intended to suit a transient state of affairs. When the latter ceased, it became self-evident that the provisional law had lost its binding force. This principle is of wide application in comparing Deuteronomy with the Levitical Code.

To both methods as presented by Delitzsch (Genes. Einl., 43, 44), Dr. Kuenen again takes exception. Delitzsch had referred to the *corpus juris Justinianeum* as a parallel, and shown by a quotation from Savigny, how jurists resort to the same principle, when the Digesta, Institutiones, and the Codex occasionally contradict each other or themselves. Kuenen remarks, "I do not believe that the Mosaic origin of the Pentateuchal Codes is made more probable by this analogy. Does not the discrepancy between the various parts of the *corpus juris* arise from the origin of its laws in various periods? If, therefore, the case be the same with the Pentateuch, the successive origin of the Mosaic Codes becomes highly probable." This retort of his own argument upon Delitzsch would be justified if we had the same historical testimony for the gradual origination of the Mosaic institutions as there is for the development of Roman law. The opposite of this is true. And Dr. Kuenen overlooks, that the point of analogy consists simply in the fact that a Code may be in operation of which the individual laws seem to contradict each other. What may be the cause of this discrepancy is not the question here: it is enough that the fact be verified. If the *corpus juris* was valid law at a certain time, why not the Mosaic law also? And if it be proven that the variations in the former are due to diversity of origin, we will wait till the same evidence is presented for the Mosaic laws. The contradictions in themselves do not prove anything as long as—

(*a*) They can be harmonized.

(*b*) The difference explained on other grounds.

(*c*) The positive proof that they owe their origin to diversity of authorship is not given.

We cannot enter here upon the discussion of individual cases, most of which will, moreover, come up at later points of our inquiry. And it can be confidently claimed that all of them have met with a satisfactory solution long ago.

With regard to repetitions, a few remarks may suffice: —

1. The objection based on the frequent restatement of essentially the same law, disregards the peculiar relation in which the living God stood to his Covenant-people Israel. He was the great Law-giver and Theocratic King, but at the same time the father of his subjects; and where he had to command in the former capacity, he could urge and beseech repeatedly in the latter.

2. The Pentateuch, as a whole, is not a legal Code, but a history of the foundation of the Theocracy. What may be less appropriate in an official Code, becomes quite natural in its historical environment.

3. The character of the repeated laws affords an easy explanation of this fact. Most of them are of the highest importance for Israel's religious life. As an example, we may refer to the Sabbatical laws. Not less than eleven substantially the same are found in Exodus-Numbers.

4. Very few actual repetitions exist where the subject is not approached in every new treatment from a different side, or with the purpose to introduce some modification.

Chapter Seven - Development of Law

By far the most formidable objection raised by modern critics against the unity of the Pentateuchal Codes, rests on the assertion that they betray by their contents and form a natural growth from the simple to the complex, and that their various parts represent each a different stage of religious development, and fit exactly into the historical periods to which their origin is respectively ascribed. This evolutionary theory, of course, has led to the reconstruction of the whole Jewish history. If the essence of the Christian conception of revelation consist in a direct interference of God, the creation of a new order of things, the implanting by an act of grace of what nature had become unable to produce; if the perfect and absolute stand here at the beginning, and are the source, not the fruit, of all development,—then it will surely follow that a naturalistic philosophy must end with the beginning, and begin with the end. The difference must needs be radical. Whosoever, like Dr. Kuenen, rules out the supernatural element from Israel's history cannot occupy a halfway position: he will place the contents of revelation at the end, because, at every other point, their interpolation would disturb the order of development.

The law according to Wellhausen is an accommodation to the natural tendencies of the people. Originally the ceremonial cultus was rooted in the soil of heathen nature-worship, and in its primitive form it was the spontaneous expression of a natural religious impulse. To the first part of his Prolegomena, treating the history of the cultus, he has prefixed the motto, *Legem non habentes natura faciunt legis opera*. What distinguished Israel from the Gentiles was not its ceremonial institutions,—rather the opposite; for "the cultus is the heathen element in the Jewish religion." Only after the codification and systematizing of these primitive elements during and after the exile, did the law become the exponent of the people's peculiar character. First, prophecy had raised its powerful voice in opposition to all outward rites, as being rooted in, closely allied to, and in necessary connection with, the worship of other gods. Pure Jahveism in a spiritual sense was the ideal which the prophets continually held up before the people, without being able to realize it amongst them. How we shall account for the sudden appearance of a class of men with such spiritual ideas and lofty aspirations, among a people scarcely awakened out of the mystic sleep of Oriental nature-worship, to the first faint consciousness of something more definite and personal, we ask in vain. The fact is surely not less miraculous and astounding than the promulgation of a divine law on Sinai. But the prophetical voice so powerfully raised at first, became weaker and weaker, and at last was silenced entirely. Spiritualism had taken up arms against ritualism, and lost the battle. Seeing that it could not successfully resist this natural tendency of Israel, it began to accommodate its demands to the desires of the people, and tried to assimilate the essentially heathen elements to its own Jahvistic ideas; and by this strange but dexterous renouncement of former principles, the strongest obstacle in the way of Jahvistic monotheism was all at once transformed into its most powerful incentive and reliable safeguard. What happened, according to Wellhausen, finds an illustration in the methods followed by the Christian Church, in adopting heathen practices and customs, and making them the symbols of Christian facts and ideas.

It is true this scheme presents a difficulty which has not entirely escaped the critics themselves. Wellhausen confesses that the Levitical Theocracy indicates a retrogressive movement in the religious growth of Israel. He characterizes the introduction of the Pentateuchal Codes as a systematic relapse into that heathenism which the prophets had condemned and opposed with all their might. There is a break in the process here. Prophetism had proclaimed spiritual Jahveism, and condemned ritualism instead of adhering to this vital principle (its only *raison d'être*), and exalting the idea above the form, which was the true import of its mission, it now forsakes the essential and spiritual aim of all its striving, satisfied if merely the form be saved, if only a sort of Jahveism, be it ever so gross and superstitious and ceremonial, be preserved.

Not all critics agree as to the precise order in which the several portions of the various Codes originated. As to the Codes themselves, the most favorite succession is that proposed by the reconstructionists of Wellhausen's type, being Covenant-law, Deuteronomy, Ezekiel's Program, Priest Code. Graf distributes the legal contents of the Pentateuch in the following way—

1. The Jehovistic recension of the Elohistic narrative (which he assigns to the time of King Ahaz) contained Exod. 13, 20-23, 34.

2. The law-book discovered in the eighteenth year of King Josiah, and written during his reign, contained Deut. 4:45-28:69. Of this, however, chap. 21-25 belong to an earlier time, and formed originally a supplement to the laws of Exodus. Graf is inclined to identify the Deuteronomist with Jeremiah.

3. Ezekiel is the author of Lev. 18-26, and of the Sabbath-law in Exod. 31.

4. In the time of Ezra, and probably by Ezra himself, were written Exod. 12:1-28, 43-51; 25-31 and 35-40; Lev. 1-16 (only chap. 11 contains an older law), 24:10-23; Num. 1:48-10:28, 15-19, 28-31, 35:16-36:13.

5. Soon after the time of Ezra the whole was completed by the addition of Lev. 27 and some minor parts.

Since the latest schemes place Deuteronomy between the Covenant-book and the Levitical laws, we must anticipate some parts of our discussion. The historical side of the problem will also come here, already more or less under consideration.

Chapter Eight - Unity, or Plurality, of Sanctuary?

It is alleged, that before the Deuteronomic reform and the centralization which it effected, sacrifices were offered, even by the most pious Israelites, at all places throughout the land, specially on the Bamoth, or high places, to which a peculiar sanctity was ascribed. The Covenant-law is claimed to testify to this state of affairs; and the classical passage, Exod. 20:24-26, is generally quoted as decisive for the view, that, long after the conquest of the land, a plurality of sanctuaries was not only tolerated, but legalized.

All will, of course, depend on the exegesis of this passage; and the latter will be determined by the context. As we have hitherto discovered no evidence of the composite character of the Codes, we vindicate our right to interpret these verses in the light of what precedes and follows. Thus viewing them, we would state their bearing on the present question under the following heads: —

1. They contain simply some provisional directions: —

(a) For the altar to be erected for the Covenant-sacrifice (Exod. 24).

(b) For all sacrifices to be offered before the tabernacle was ready (compare also Josh. 8:31).

The only objections that can be reasonably urged against this natural explanation are the following two:—

(1) The time between the promulgation of this command and the erection of the tabernacle was too short to require a special provision.

According to Exod. 40:1, the tabernacle was not reared before the first day of the first month of the second year after the exodus. And even then the tabernacle-service could not go into effect, because the sacrificial laws had not yet been given. Not before Lev. 8 do we find the command to consecrate Aaron and his sons (compare also Num. 1:1). Thus the time between the publication of this command and the inauguration of the tabernacle-service was at least eight full months. Were the children of Israel without sacrifices all this time? If not, and if each was his own priest, and built his own altar, what was more natural than a provision of this character? Afterwards, of course, it was partially abrogated by the fuller and permanent arrangement of the ritual system.

(2) The directions that the altar should be of unhewn stone, and that it should not he ascended by steps, are claimed to be of general character, and thus to preclude the subsequent promulgation of the Levitical law, which contradicts them.

As to the first of these points, we claim on our side that the command is not general, but special and temporary. Because the altar which each man would build for himself could not be consecrated, it should consist of simple, undefiled, natural material. Of course, to the altar of the tabernacle, made according to God's own prescriptions, solemnly consecrated and served by an official priesthood, these restrictions did not apply.

The prohibition to ascend the altar by steps, had in it an element of permanent validity, as ver. 26 intimates. Only the special way in which this necessity was met, had no perpetual binding force. Hence, whilst the Levitical law preserved the former, it could disregard the latter. The principle was maintained, but in the manner stated in Exod. 28:42, 39:28.

2. The critics cannot satisfactorily account for the addition, "where I record my name." Wellhausen dismisses the significant phrase with the following insignificant remark: "This only means that the place of communion between heaven and earth is not to be regarded as arbitrarily chosen, but as in some way designated by God himself." The reference of this clause to the successive stations of the tabernacle during the desert-journey, is not excluded, but does not do full justice to the meaning. It is intended that all places become sacred by a manifestation of God, whether it be in a theophany, or by the Shechinah, or in some other way. On Sinai, God recorded his name in a glorious revelation and thus to the Israelites the provisional right could be given to build an altar there. Afterwards, when the manifestation of God's glory was transferred to the tent of the testimony, this of necessity became the only recognized sanctuary. The passage clearly intimates, that, as often as altered circumstances would in the future render centralization of worship practically impossible, the same freedom would be restored, always, of course, with the same restriction, that no place of sacrifice should be arbitrarily chosen, but only such as were sanctified by "a recording of God's name." Actually, we find in subsequent history that all such consecrated spots had been the scene of a theophany: they were so many "Sinais," where the same command could be repeated, and the pious Israelite once more erect his simple altar of earth or unhewn stone, and sacrifice his burnt-offering and peace-offering, his sheep and oxen.

That the Covenant-law positively presupposes unity of worship and cultus, is seen from the feast-laws, Exod. 23:17, 19, where every male is required to appear three times in the year before the LORD God. If the sanctuaries were so numerous as the critics assert, and accordingly visited continually and frequently by all Israelites, a command like this, to appear *three times* before the LORD, would have been superfluous and unmeaning.

We see that the attempt to bring the Covenant-law into contradiction with the subsequent Codes, or to show that it sanctions a more primitive form of sanctuary-worship, rests on a very forced interpretation of a single passage severed from its context. That there was a relative element in this regulation, is absurd to deny; and the absolute principles involved were retained, though in a somewhat modified form, in the Levitical law, so that no discrepancy exists. Surely no development of centuries was required to effect the unessential difference between these verses and the description of the altar in the tabernacle, modifications which are fully accounted for by the historical situation that conditioned both.

It is further alleged that this first Code makes no provision for the priests and their support, and thus silently assumes the common right of all Israelites to offer sacrifice. We deny that the latter proposition can be logically deduced from the former; and as to the silence of the Code, if the argument. proves any thing, it proves that there was no privileged priesthood as late as the time of David or Jehoshaphat, which is more than even the most destructive critics are willing to assert. The *argumentum e silentio* has no force unless it be shown, that to legislate on this topic fell within the scope and purpose of this law. It regulates simply the Covenant-relation between Jehovah and his people. Shall we conclude from the silence as to circumcision and leprosy, and many other topics, that these were unknown in the tenth or ninth century? But we have no more right to draw any inference from the fact that no priests are mentioned here. Moreover, an evidently prospective statement is made (Exod. 24:1, 9) concerning Aaron, Nadab, and Abihu, who are commanded with Moses to come up to the LORD. By this distinction they are singled out from the rest of the people; and on no other ground could this distinction of Aaron's sons have been made, than in view of their future priesthood, and their appearing before God in the tabernacle.

Deuteronomy is quoted as testifying to the actual state of affairs during the transition period immediately before the centralization under Josiah. It contains, we are told, the reminiscences of what the Covenant-law represented as indispensable reality. The Deuteronomist writes throughout in a polemic tone, and assumes the character of a reformer. It indicates certainly no great concession when we admit that the Deuteronomic Code enforces and inculcates unity of worship more than any thing else. To draw from this the direct inference, that it must be both the product of, and the norm for, the reaction against Bamoth-worship in the latter part of the seventh century B.C., is very hasty and sweeping. What the critics may be called upon to prove, is not that Deuteronomy had a striking fitness to serve as a reform-Code in the days of King Josiah. Nobody denies this, and there is abundant evidence that it was actually used thus. Neither will the evidence that the Code could accomplish a greater and more important mission in the seventh century than in the Mosaic time, justify the conclusion that it owes its origin to the former, and not to the latter. God did not inspire his holy word for a single age or generation: it never returneth void, but accomplishes sooner or later all that which he pleases. The one and the essential point which we wish the higher criticism to establish, is this, that the Code does not fit into the historical situation, by which, according to its own testimony, it was called forth. As far as we know, this has never been done. The two preceding points have been settled, which it required surely no higher criticism to do; but we object to a use of them as if they warranted an inference that can only be drawn from the third. Is there any impropriety in the tone and contents of the book, when we realize that the Israelites were to enter upon the possession of a land, for centuries defiled by a heathen cultus that almost every high place would by its associations expose them to the utmost danger of relapsing into idolatry and nature-worship? If ever a time called for an urgent appeal to the people to maintain the centralization of their cultus as a safeguard against Canaanitish influences, it was the latter part of the Mosaic period. And the remarkable fact, that Deuteronomy emphasizes as much the permanence of the once established sanctuary as its unity, suits far better the Mosaic time than the seventh century, when the thought that the temple could be removed from Jerusalem would have been considered absurd. Entirely too much has been made of the frequently recurring expressions: "the place which the LORD your God shall choose (יִבְחַר) out of all your tribes to put (שׂוּם) his name there (לְשַׁכֵּן)." Riehm asserts that this could not have been spoken by Moses with reference to the uncertain place of the tabernacle. But here criticism, otherwise so averse to prophetic foresight, seems to claim for Moses a minute knowledge of the future fate of the sanctuary. What else could Moses expect than that, after the conquest of Canaan, a definite place would be chosen by God to dwell there, either in tabernacle or temple? Even long after the Mosaic age, in the same time to which critics ascribe the origin of Deuteronomy, all these terms were applied to the tabernacle and its locality by Jer. 7:12. בְּשִׁילוֹ אֲשֶׁר שִׁכַּנְתִּי שְׁמִי.

So much about the prospective character of Deuteronomy. Since it has a retrospective side also, we must briefly inquire whether this lends stronger support to the critical view. Does Deuteronomy paint the past with such colors as compel us to postulate between it and the Covenant-law a period of at least two centuries?

We are referred chiefly to such expressions as the following: "Ye shall not do after all the things that we do here this day, every man whatsoever is right in his own eyes" (12:8, *seqq.*). Deuteronomy, it is said, "opposes consciously" "what we are now accustomed to do." Its reform is not merely modifying but condemning, previous legislation, not only reformatory, but polemic. And to explain this marked difference between it and the Jehovist, a considerable interval of time must be assumed. It is impossible, if the Covenant-law had been promulgated at Sinai and Deuteronomy in the plains of Moab, that the latter should condemn what the former had approved of.

In answer to this we remark, —

1. The promulgation of the Levitical Code, which according to our view falls between the Covenant-law and Deuteronomy, has been overlooked here by the critics. The tabernacle represented absolute unity of worship; and, this having been abandoned in the desert, it is not strange that Deuteronomy condemns in the most polemic terms a subsequent relapse into previous customs, which had now become unallowable.

2. That such a subsequent relapse took place during the thirty-eight years of wandering in the desert under the judgment of God, is proved by historical testimony, not only that of the Pentateuch, but also of Amos 5:25, 26. Whatever may be the more definite exegesis of this difficult passage, it doubtless alludes to such a state of affairs as Deuteronomy condemns. It is true that Amos does not directly charge the Israelites with having sacrificed in a plurality of places at the same time, but only that they had "taken up the tabernacle of Moloch and Chiun their images, the star of their god, which they made to themselves." But it is clear that the former is a direct inference from the latter statement. Unity of worship stood and fell with pure Jahveism, of which the central idea is the recognition of one personal God, to whom belongs the initiative in all that pertains to his service. The moment this definite and exclusive idea is lost, there returns with the vague conceptions of nature-worship, the unlimited freedom to sacrifice at all places where this uncircumscribed deity of nature reveals itself; i.e., everywhere. That the idolatry to which Amos refers was conducted throughout the camp, and not centralized in the tabernacle, admits of no doubt; and this alone furnishes a sufficient ground for the polemical tone of Deuteronomy. For it is true of the past as well as of the future, that the prophet's eye takes in more than a single day: it covers periods, and sees them in the light of their most significant features. Hence the prophet Moses, looking back upon the last forty years, could even in the fields of Moab, at the dawn of a new period, truthfully say, "Not as we are *now* accustomed to do."

3. The protest against a plurality of places of sacrifice is brought into close connection throughout the Code with the warning against heathen idolatry (Deut. 12:2, 3, and so *passim*). But the critics are emphatic in telling us that Bamoth-worship was Jahveh-worship. Accordingly, this feature suits the Mosaic period far better than the age of the later Judaic kings. The dark future and the still darker past combined in these days of Moses to inspire him with fear for Israel's corrupt tendencies in this direction.

4. That Deuteronomy in its general representations often approaches very closely to the later times, proves nothing more than that we have here an example of generic prophecy. These later evils were the natural results of the dangers to which Israel was exposed in the midst of a heathen environment. It did not require a great amount of supernatural foresight to discern them beforehand. And all critics admit that Deuteronomy, on the whole, has a prophetic character. How can it awake our surprise, that the prescription of a general remedy for a general class of evils was found appropriate as often and as late as the occasion or the necessity required?

5. We close with the remark, that in view of the striking resemblance between the Mosaic time and the state of religion in the seventh century, and the almost perfect fitting of Deuteronomy into the historical circumstances of both, it must surprise us, that the critics have not been bold enough to reject the whole history of Israel's apostasy, and wandering in the desert, as a "his-

torical fiction," a new and unprecedented example of carrying back the present into the past with a Jesuitical intention. If the attempt has been successful in the case of the tabernacle, we do not see why it should not be practicable here. But if there are so many temptations to reiterate the bold hypothesis, and nevertheless the stern reality of history would not allow them, it may well serve us as a warning not to yield too readily to similar facts, presented in the same attractive light, wherewith a little less historical testimony, the critics have actually risked the dangerous step of proclaiming that the history of the past is but an embellished reproduction of a subsequent present. We are content to call neither a counterfeit of the other, but to find in both the genuine reflection, which in all times and all places the invariable methods of God's dealing with men will produce in the mirror of history.

According to Wellhausen, there is no other difference between Deuteronomy and the Priest Code on this point than that the latter takes for granted what the former requires. With regard to a second point closely allied to the one just discussed, the case stands different. We must, in the second place, examine the pretended development of the sacrificial system.

Chapter Nine - The Sacrificial System

Here the Jehovist and Deuteronomist go together, and stand diametrically opposed to Ezekiel and the Priest Code. And even within the limits of the Priest Code itself, an expansion of the ceremonial is traceable. Wellhausen makes substantially the following statements: —

1. According to the Jehovist and the Deuteronomist, sacrifices are a universal and extremely simple means of honoring the Deity, and conciliating his favor. They are pre-Mosaic, and along the line of Jacob, Isaac, Abraham, Noah, go back to the beginnings of humanity, to Cain and Abel. The Elohist, on the other hand, represents the sacrificial worship as an immediate divine institution, characteristically Mosaic in origin.

2. With the Jehovist and in Deuteronomy the important question is, "To whom?" The Elohist emphasizes the questions, "When, where, and by whom?" In other words, the Jehovist has not, and the Elohist has, an elaborate program of ritual.

3. In the Jehovistic and Deuteronomic Codes, no other than burnt-offerings (*olah*) and peace- (or thank-) offerings (*shelem, zebah, zebah shelamim*) appear. Moreover, the *olah* constitutes no separate class for itself, but is simply the substitute in a large zebah (consisting of several animals) of a single whole victim for all the pieces of fat and the blood, otherwise offered to God, of each individual animal. Hence *olah* occurs almost always in connection with the *zebahim* in the singular number. That part of every *zebah* which came upon the altar (fat and blood) could appropriately be called *olah*. Still, Wellhausen admits that the term is never used in this sense, but always denotes a ὁλόκαυστον. In Ezekiel and the Priest Code the order is reversed, and

zebah has become subordinate to the *olah*. The altar is called *mizbah-ha-olah* (the altar of burnt-offering). Two new kinds of sacrifices are added, — *chattath* (sin-offering) and *asham* (trespass-offering).

4. It is claimed that we have a gradual modification of the idea of sacrifice.

(*a*) The primitive conception is that of a meal in which the Deity is host, and the offerer a guest. Sacrifices are identical with sacrificial meals.

(*b*) Next comes the *shelem* (peace-offering) of the Priest Code with a reminiscence of the old custom, in so far as the sacrificial meal is retained. The modification consists in the giving of the breast and the right shoulder to the priest. This is a first restriction upon the conception of a meal.

(*c*) Then follows the *olah* (burnt-offering) of the Priest Code. Here also the priests have their part in the skin. The whole victim is burnt upon the altar, which still admits the conception of a one-sided meal, consumed by God alone.

(*d*) In the *chattath* (sin-offering) and *asham* (trespass-offering), even this is lost; since none of the flesh is brought upon the altar, but the whole eaten by the priests. All that could remind of a sacrificial meal, as flour, oil, wine, salt, is wanting; so that the last trace of the original idea is effaced.

5. As an example of modification within the limits of the Priest Code itself, stands the case of the offering of incense and altar of incense. The latter is unknown to the older parts of the Code, not mentioned among the utensils of the tabernacle, Exod. 25-29, but spoken of at the end, in a separate passage, evidently of later origin (30:1, etc.). The rite of the most solemn sin-offering, according to Exod. 29, Lev. 8 and 9, was not performed at this altar. On the Day of Atonement, Aaron offers incense, not on the altar, but in a censer before the mercy-seat within the veil. So also Lev. 10, Num. 16, 17. In all these chapters, the altar of burnt-offering is called *ha-mizbeah*, which precludes the existence of another altar. In the later sections of the Pentateuchal Code, the name *mizbah-ha-olah* appears; and these are exactly the passages which know the altar of incense. This whole idea of a golden altar was an after-development from that of the golden table of show-bread. Other points in which a development is traceable are mentioned by Wellhausen; e.g., the flour first used was קֶמַח (*meal*), the Priest Code demands סֹלֶת (*fine flour*). The old custom of boiling the meat gave place to roasting, — a refinement in the rite, of course, arising from a refinement of the eater's taste.

With reference to all these points, we would remark, —

1. If Deuteronomy lays so much stress on the centralization of the cultus, it would be naturally expected, provided this were the formative principle of the development, as Wellhausen claims, that a corresponding change would be noticeable in its sacrificial prescriptions. This, however, is, not the case. We have Wellhausen's own confession that Deuteronomy falls in with the Jehovist on the whole line. This is a clear proof that the alleged discrepancies are not to be explained on the principle of development, but out of the peculiar aim of each Code in particular. In Deuteronomy, to say the least, we have

positive proof that the two conceptions of sacrifice — that of a ceremonial act bound to a single place, and that of a joyful meal — are not exclusive, but mutually supplement each other.

2. The contrast that the Jehovistic legislation is only concerned with the question "to whom?" and the Priest Code exclusively emphasizes, "how, when, where, and by whom?" is by far too sharply drawn. We find with the Jehovist, provisions in the latter direction (Exod. 20:24-26, 23:18, 19). On the contrary, the Levitical law enforces principles which, according to the critics, are Jehovistic (e.g., Lev. 19:4, 5, 20:1-5).

3. That sacrifices were originally extremely simple in their ritual, and pre-Mosaic in their essential features, does not prove any thing against the Mosaic origin of the Priest Code. The Levitical law nowhere asserts that Moses for the first time instituted sacrifices: it simply states that the ritual system, as adapted to Israel's new position as God's Covenant-people, dates from the Mosaic period.

4. That the *olah* did not originally constitute a separate class of sacrifices for itself, requires stronger proof than Wellhausen has been able to produce. All that he shows, is that *olah* and *zebahim* were frequently combined. This, however, is also the case in the Priest Code. The impossibility of considering the *olah* as a subordinate part of the *zebah* is manifest; because the fat and blood of an individual *zebah* are never called *olah*, as Wellhausen is obliged to admit. The term is exclusively employed of whole-burnt offerings, ὁλόκαυστα. It is plain, then, that the specific difference lies not in the coming upon the altar: in other words, *olah* and *zebah* are *essentially* distinct.

5. It is true that in the Jehovistic Code, only burnt- and peace-offerings are mentioned (Exod. 20:24, 24:5). But, on the one hand, nothing can be inferred from two passages: on the other hand, as the Levitical Code had not yet been promulgated, the Covenant-law retained provisionally the older practice and *ritus.*

6. Concerning Wellhausen's denial of the actual existence of the altar of incense, we remark, —

(*a*) It cannot be maintained that Exod. 30:1-10 is out of place, and proves itself by this position a later appendix. The description of the utensils of the tabernacle began with the ark, and ended with the altar of incense; because both constituted, as it were, the two polar points of the sanctuary. Hence the altar is called קֹדֶשׁ קָדָשִׁים (*Holy of holies*), in preference to the candlestick, and table of showbread.

(*b*) That the altar is not mentioned in connection with the most solemn rite described in Exod. 29 (consecration of the priests commanded), Lev. 8 (the same executed), and Lev. 9 (entrance of Aaron and his sons upon their actual service), need not surprise us when we remember, that in all these cases, the priests, while still undergoing the rite of consecration, are not treated as priests. Hence the prescription of Lev. 4, to put some of the blood upon the horns of the altar of incense, did not apply here; because, *de facto*, Aaron was not a high-priest as long as the induction to his office lasted. Only for the sin-offering of the high-priest and the whole congregation, was the blood put upon the altar of incense (Lev. 4:22, *seqq.*).

(*c*) When, according to Lev. 16, Aaron on the Day of Atonement brought incense in a censer before the mercy-seat, we surely could not expect him to have carried the heavy altar within the veil. And that coals are taken from the altar of burnt-offering is equally natural. Even the fire for the daily offering of incense was taken from this altar. The only remaining difficulty is, that in chap. 16 only one altar is mentioned as being sprinkled with blood. "The altar that is before the LORD" seems to denote the *olah* altar. Universal tradition has referred it to the altar of incense; and so does Delitzsch (Luth. Zeitschr., 1880, iii. p. 118), who adds the remark, that the name is exclusively used of the golden altar in the holy place. The context, however, plainly contradicts this: from ver. 14-20 the order is the same as in the recapitulation of ver. 33. In the latter verse the altar cannot but designate the *olah* altar. Accordingly we must understand ver. 18 in the same sense. The chapter distinguishes throughout between (*a*) the holy place (here the Holy of holies), (*b*) the tabernacle of the congregation, (*c*) the altar that is before the LORD, which can only mean the altar in the court.

The true explanation why the altar of incense is not specially mentioned, is that it was included under the general term, "the tabernacle of the congregation," together with the candlestick and table of showbread. On the contrary, the *olah* altar is marked out, because it was the only thing in the court to be atoned for. The phrase "before the LORD" is evidently intended in a wider sense here, to denote that the altar of burnt-offering stood in front of the whole tabernacle, God's dwelling-place.

(*d*) Lev. 10 and Num. 16, 17, as extraordinary or unlawful transactions, do not come under consideration here.

(*e*) It is untrue that the name *ha-mizbeah,* applied to the *olah* altar, precludes the existence of another altar. The former could be appropriately designated by that name, because it was the place of sacrifice, if not exclusively, yet par excellence.

(*f*) No more difficulty is created by the fact, that those sections of the Pentateuch which show acquaintance with the altar of incense, use the more definite name for the *olah* altar, whilst those which do not know the former, call the latter ha-*mizbeah*. The simple explanation is, that, in passages where both altars are referred to, a closer distinction was necessary to prevent confusion. In other passages, where only the *olah* altar was mentioned, this was superfluous, and the simple name ha-*mizbeah* was sufficient to indicate that the altar *par excellence* was meant.

(*g*) Wellhausen alleges that the idea of a golden altar is a mere development of that of the golden table of showbread, and finds confirmation for this theory in Ezek. 41:22. "The altar of wood," etc.; "this is the table that is before the Lord." The fact is, that in Ezekiel's sanctum, neither candlestick nor table of show-bread appears, — which once more proves how absurd it is, to draw from his Thora any inference as to the state of the ritual in his days. The statement in ver. 22 applies to nothing else than to the very altar whose existence Wellhausen denies. It is certainly more probable that the prophet called the altar a table, than the table an altar. The designation of the altar as a table is warranted by post-exilic usage. Furthermore, Ezekiel clearly distinguishes two altars in the temple (9:2).

Chapter Ten - Priests and Levites

Our next point of inquiry concerns the priests and Levites, and their relation to each other. Critics claim that in no point is the development more clearly traceable step by step than here. By a gradual restriction, the priestly office became the exclusive prerogative of the so-called sons of Aaron. Ezek. 44:6-11 describes the degradation of the great mass of Levites from priests to temple-servants, and is the bridge between Deuteronomy, which recognizes all Levites as priests, and uses the two terms interchangeably, on the one hand, and the Priest Code on the other hand, where only the Sons of Aaron are allowed to appear before Jahveh. According to 1 Kings 2:27, 35, Abiathar was removed by Solomon from the priesthood for political reasons, and replaced by Zadok, whose descendants from that time onward seem to have monopolized the temple-service. As Deuteronomy shows, in the days of King Josiah the Levites could still claim an equal right to this service. The distinction between the sons of Zadok and the other Levites was not one of rank, but simply of actual service. Accordingly we find them in juxtaposition in statements like the following: צָדוֹק וְכָל־הַלְוִיִם (*Zadok and all the Levites*), 2 Sam 15:24 (Graf, p. 48). Only within the circle of the sons of Zadok themselves, Graf admits that there may have been a certain gradation in rank, from the lowest temple-servant upward to the כֹּהֵן הַגָּדוֹל or כֹּהֵן הָרֹאשׁ (*high-priest*), 2 Kings 12:11, 22:4, 8; Jer. 20:1. With the centralization of Deuteronomy, the seed for the future distinction of rank was sown. The Levitical priests of the province, separated from their altars, could no longer remain priests. Deuteronomy still puts them on a par with the sons of Zadok; but the latter had long ceased to consider them as equals, and now began to question their rights altogether. This was the actual state of affairs, which Ezekiel tries to present in a moral light. He reproves the idolatrous ministering of the Levites as priests at the Bamoth; and, in punishment for this iniquity, they are degraded to temple-servants. Thus they shall atone for what was most abominable in the prophet's estimation, and henceforward the Levites exist as an order distinct from the priests. Notwithstanding this moral semblance, it is clear that Ezekiel's retributive justice was of a peculiar retrogressive kind: he proclaims as a punishment what had long ago been the real situation, and was after all but a natural consequence of the centralization. What the prophet did, was to settle the controversy between Levites and Zadokites in favor of the latter. He did not claim for the house of Zadok, Aaronic descent, because in his days it was well known that the old line had ceased during the reign of Solomon. Not until after the exile, when the thread of tradition had been lost, could the Priest Code present this claim, and the chronicler establish it by a series of artificial genealogies.

We have accordingly in this development the following stages —

1. Jehovistic Code. No mention of priests. Young men offer sacrifices (Exod. 24:3-8). A priestly order, but no priestly family.

2. Deuteronomy recognizes a hereditary *clerus* consisting of numerous families with exclusive and indisputable privileges. Also the name "Levitical priests" appears. The principle of heredity, though afterwards carried back into the Mosaic age, actually dates from the later times of the kingdom, and was entirely Judaic in origin.

3. Ezekiel legalizes the distinction between the priestly family connected with the temple and the families before connected with the Bamoth. This distinction had long been valid as a matter of fact; viz., ever since the Bamoth were destroyed. Now, however, it is clothed with divine authority.

4. What Ezekiel saw it necessary to justify as a divinely authenticated innovation, the Priest Code finds it possible to proclaim as an "eternal statute." Reminiscences of opposition appear in the history of Korah's rebellion (compare also Num. 17:10, 18:23). Here we have the regular gradation in descending order: Aaron as high-priest, his sons as priests, his tribe as Levites, constitute a systematic hierarchy. In pre-exilic history and literature, an imposing figure like that of the high-priest was wholly unknown. The priesthood was rather a royal dependency. But in the Priest Code the high-priest is sovereign, the top of the pyramid of Israel's congregation reaching into heaven, and unto Jahveh himself. A theocratic king beside him is unthinkable. That the head of the cultus is at the same time head of the nation, points us to a time when the nation was robbed of its secular independence, and had nothing left but its ecclesiastical organization. Israel has become a congregation, עֵדָה. Dependence on foreign power is the necessary prerequisite for the origin of a hierarchy. Hence the Priest Code must be post-exilic.

In commenting upon this ingenious theory, it will be necessary more than once to cast a side-glance at the historical arguments by which it is fortified. Our remarks are the following:—

1. It is positively untrue that the Jehovistic law knows nothing of a priestly order. That it is only occasionally alluded to, and not repeatedly mentioned, cannot awake suspicion: for (*a*) it did not exist when the Covenant-law was promulgated; (*b*) the purpose of this law was not to regulate the ritual system, but simply to furnish a basis on which it could be constructed. On the other hand, that incidental allusions and prospective remarks should be made in reference to the subject can be expected. The following passages, which are Jehovistic, fully warrant us in saying that the Covenant-law is not

contradictory to, but rather preparatory for, the more full Levitical legislation (Exod. 4:14, 19:22, 32:1, 29, 33:7-11). Wellhausen rules out such passages from the list of arguments by mere capricious remarks like the following "Exod. 32:29 stands on the basis of Deuteronomy," and "Exod. 19:22 can hardly (?) have belonged to the original Jehovistic sources" (Prolegomena, 2d ed., p. 146).

2. It is inaccurate, also, to say that Deuteronomy puts the priests and Levites on a par. No argument for this can be drawn from the absence of a strongly marked and everywhere emphasized distinction. As we hope to show hereafter, this absence is wholly in accordance with the general character of the book. Moreover, Deuteronomy does not aim to give complete or precisely formulated directions, but only compact popular restatements of matters minutely regulated elsewhere. That the author speaks of Levites in general in not a few passages, where, more accurately expressed, the priests are meant, must be explained on the rule, that the genus may be used to designate the species, where there is no danger of ambiguity. The same inaccuracy occurs in the historical books (compare Josh. 3:3, 8:33, 13:14, 18:7; 1 Sam. 2:27; 2 Chron. 5:5, 30:27): even Malachi, who wrote after the pretended promulgation of the Priest Code, speaks in the same manner (2:4). The priests were Levites in reality. Is it not natural that in the middle books of the Pentateuch, in laws enacted while yet Aaron and his sons occupied the priestly office, the priests should have been designated by the familiar term "sons of Aaron" and that afterwards, when both Aaron and two of his sons had died, in a book of prophetic character, the more general term "Levitical priests" should have been chosen, denoting "those Levites who shall be priests at any time of the future"? The lack of definiteness in Deuteronomy, where it employs these terms, cannot be construed as proving entire ignorance of the distinction. The passage (Deut. 18:1) is instructive in this respect. Graf and other critics hold that "Levites" stands here in apposition to "priests," and the expression "all the tribe of Levi" to "priests (and) Levites." On this critical presupposition we have three terms to express that which each of them separately would have expressed with sufficient clearness, so that at least two are superfluous. Under these circumstances we are certainly justified in taking an alternative, and considering the construction as an *asyndeton:* "The Levitical priests (and) the whole tribe of Levi," which is in full accordance with the context. In ver. 5, if the priesthood of the whole tribe was presupposed, we would naturally expect "him (the priest) and his brethren for ever." The phrase "him and his *sons*" strikes us as more suitable to a hereditary priesthood within a single family, than to the existence of a priestly tribe.

Other instances of this generic designation of the priests occur in the Old Testament, even in books written after the exile, which cannot but have known the distinction between Levites and priests (Ezra 10:5; Neh. 10:28, 38, 11:20).

56

But, we are told, Deuteronomy allows the Levites "to stand before the LORD," עֲמֹד לִפְנֵי יְהֹוָה; "minister to the LORD," (אֶת יְהֹוָה) שֵׁרֵת בְּשֵׁם יְהֹוָה; "bless in the name of the LORD," בֵּרֵךְ בְּשֵׁם יְהֹוָה; all these being in the Priest Code the exclusive prerogatives of the Aaronic priests.

These expressions occur in five passages (10:8, 17:12, 18:5, 7, 21:5). In two, however, the functions referred to are predicated of the priests, no mention being made of Levites viz., 17:12 and 21:5. We have only to examine the remaining ones, 10:8, 18:5, 7. It is a remarkable fact, that in those very books, which, according to the critics, have reconstructed the history, and thus are beyond suspicion of non-conformity to the Levitical law, — that in those very books, we say, the identical expressions are applied to the Levites. How absurd it would be to infer from 2 Chron. 29:4, 5, 11, 12, where the Levites are addressed by Hezekiah as "standing before the LORD, and serving and ministering unto him," that the author of Chronicles did not distinguish between priests and Levites (compare also 2 Chron. 23:6). Why shall we make the expression to prove in Deuteronomy what it cannot prove with any possibility in Chronicles? If Deuteronomy be written before the Priest Code, then Chronicles also.

We need not deny that these phrases originally indicated a function peculiar to the priesthood, especially in the case of " עֲמֹד לִפְנֵי י " (stand before Jehovah). But it is equally plain, that they gradually assumed a looser and wider signification, which made them alike applicable to the work of both priests and Levites. The name for all service at the sanctuary was taken *a potiori* from its most honorable and important part in which the priests officiated. This fully accounts for their exclusive use in the middle books with reference to the priests, and for their modified sense in subsequent literature.

All that remains of the argument, is that in 10:8 the phrase "to bless in his name" is without any specification applied to the whole tribe of Levi. There are no other instances in which this same construction, בֵּרֵךְ with the preposition בְּ, is used, when others than priests are spoken of. Still, this is far from admitting that the verse under consideration teaches the equality of priests and Levites. The best exegesis seems to be, to take the whole verse as predicated in general of the whole tribe of Levi. Of the duties enumerated, part belonged to the Levites and priests in common, as, "to stand before the LORD," "to minister unto him"; part to the Levites especially, as the bearing of the ark; part to the priests alone, as "to bless in the LORD's name." All this was so perfectly self-evident, that no specification was needed.

3. Ezekiel's Thora is for the modern critics what his δός μοί που στῶ was for Archimedes. With their interpretation of it and the inferences drawn therefrom, the whole structure of their historical theories stands or falls. At first blush, the point would seem to have been very badly chosen for historical argumentation. The whole section is of a highly ideal character, and was

written in a time when, from historic reality, the cultus had become already a distant dream, and the prophetic idealization could accordingly be given free play. It is needless to point out in detail how many features in these chapters will not admit a historical or literal interpretation, and never received one even at the hand of the most obstinate literalist. It has been reserved for the higher criticism to handle and utilize this unwieldy material in the most sober and practical way.

In the face of their ideal, prospective character, the critics have been bold enough to make these chapters speak for the past, forgetting that the threads of historical tradition had been freely interwoven with those of bold forecast of the future, so as to form a prophetic mantle. We must remember that this is a vision, and in it Ezekiel sees only higher spiritual realities through the medium of an ever-changing and ever-growing symbolism. Though the latter had, of course, its points of contact with the present and the past, it could not be limited by them the essentially new truth, which the prophet revealed, required also new and modified forms, in which to clothe itself. It is from this point of view, that the critics should have estimated the historical significance and value of what they are accustomed to style "Ezekiel's program."

But let us grant, that there is at least a background of historical truth in the statements of Ezek. 44:5-16, with which we have here specially to deal. Do they bear out the critical theory of a degradation of some Levitical priests to temple-servants as the first origin of the legal distinction between priests and Levites?

The answer to this question can only be obtained from a careful and fair examination of the passage itself. Ezekiel makes three statements: the first contains an accusation, the second an announcement of punishment, the third confirms a privilege. 1. Uncircumcised persons have been used for menial employments in the temple. 2. Certain Levites have committed idolatry, and in punishment are henceforward to perform the same menial service, formerly done by the uncircumcised. 3. Certain Levitical priests, specified as the sons of Zadok, who have remained faithful when the others apostatized, are honored with the exclusive privilege of officiating before the Lord.

Our first remark is, that there must be more than an incidental connection in the prophet's mind between his first and second statement. It is unnatural to suppose that both are mentioned together, simply because the removal of the uncircumcised made a return of the Levites necessary, or because the punishment of the latter required the removal of the former, or finally because by a play of history both gave the prophet an occasion for ingenious combination. A more than superficial reading of the passage will convince us, that there is a deeper, more causal, connection. That the apostate Levites have to occupy the place of the uncircumcised, is for no other reason than because by their apostasy they had made the employment of the latter possible. They abandoned what was their specific duty, — viz., the ministering unto the priest in the temple, — sinned themselves, and became the cause of the defilement of the sanctuary. Hence a double penalty is inflicted 1. The destruction of their self-chosen places of worship; 2. The restitution of what had been abstracted from the sanctuary, by their becoming again temple-servants.

We regard it as settled by this interpretation, that Ezekiel does more than spread a moral mantle over historical facts. His words imply that the facts themselves had a moral quality. The Levites who served at the Bamoth had not always been there, but willfully left their original position at the only legal sanctuary.

The prophet does not further specify who these Levites were. That he calls them Levites (ver. 10) decides nothing, since his terms are not derived from their former position, but already from the future degradation he imposes. Neither does the fact that their destiny to officiate as temple-servants is considered as a punishment, prove, on the other hand, that they held a higher position at the sanctuary before. The only thing that can be said about it, is that they were Levites whether exclusively non-Aaronic, or partly Aaronic, is not stated. It is highly probable, however, that both priests and Levites, in the more strict sense of the term, were found amongst them.

The critical allegation, that they consisted of nothing else than Bamoth-priests out of occupation, rests on the arbitrary assumption, that the sons of Zadok are honored, not for their exceptional faithfulness to Jehovah, but on account of their extraordinary position. They were the priestly family for centuries in charge of the temple-worship. Hence, the critics infer, Ezekiel's approval of their attachment to Jehovah can but mean a prophetic sanction of the temple as the only legal sanctuary, and at the same time a side-attack upon all other places of worship. In other words, the sons of Zadok were not examples of a rare attachment to Jehovah, but the favored incumbents of a highly lucrative office. It was not a question of right and wrong, but of facts. If all this be true, if they were not only the original and highest, but also the exclusive, officers of the temple, our position, that the Levites now condemned to perform menial service, had once shared this privilege with the sons of Zadok, cannot be maintained. If the one party is approved simply for officiating at the temple, then the other was condemned simply for officiating at the Bamoth; and other moral considerations cannot have influenced the degradation of the latter.

The answer to the question, "For what special reason did the sons of Zadok deserve praise?" will decide every thing. *A priori* it seems improbable that the prophet should bestow upon them such a eulogy simply because they did not leave their comfortable position at the chief sanctuary of the land. It needed no great amount of self-abnegation and pious adherence to Jehovah, to make them stay where they were. But why may not their faithfulness have manifested itself in quite another way? We know from history, that the temple itself had been more than once the central seat of apostasy. Urijah was the instrument of the idolatrous lusts of King Ahaz; and, when Manasseh defiled the temple, no opposition on the part of the priests is so much as heard of. That such abominations were not uncommon, even after Josiah's reform, the prophet's vision in chap. 8 sufficiently shows. Hence there is all reasonable ground to assume that the merit of the sons of Zadok consisted in something more than a matter-of-fact serving in the Jerusalem temple. They evidently had remained faithful when others, occupying the same or similar privileges with them, had gone astray. And, instead of an objection, we may find in this high praise, with which their conduct is extolled, a confirmation of our view that others had abandoned that same trust, which they had so faithfully and piously kept.

This explains how Ezekiel with the Priest Code and all before him could still make a degradation out of that which the critics have declared to be explicable only on their suppositions. The whole solution lies in the fact, that Perhaps many of the apostates had been priests in the temple before. They had left the central sanctuary, and sought the Bamoth. In the reform of Josiah they lost their position. Now, in this ideal vision, Ezekiel describes their degradation from priests, which they had once been lawfully, and afterwards illegally, to Levites.

But is not this an objection to our view, that certainly the majority of these priests of the Bamoth must have been originally Levites? How in *their* case will the punishment apply? Can the restoration to a previous state after apostasy be called a penalty for the latter? In rashly answering these questions in the negative, the critics have found a tempting occasion to display their sarcasm. Dr. Kuenen asks, "How can common citizens be threatened with the penalty that henceforward they shall have no seat and vote in a council of noblemen?" But what if these citizens had either legally or illegally possessed for a considerable time this right of vote and session? When they were afterwards deprived of these in punishment of their intrusion, could anybody take exception to such a penalty? The case is not different here. The Levites had probably left the temple, aspiring to a higher position; viz., that of priests. As such they had officiated at the Bamoth. When these are destroyed, their punishment is made to consist in the disgraceful and humiliating re-entrance upon functions which in self-exalting pride they had left. What is there inappropriate in all this?

Still, it will be said that the deposed priests must have gladly accepted the most humble charge, and that so, after all, the punishment was turned into a favor, and failed to reach its end. History, however, testifies to the contrary. At the first return from the captivity under Zerubbabel and Joshua, forty-two hundred and eighty-nine priests, and only three hundred and forty-one Levites, joined the expedition. At the second, under Ezra, only thirty-eight Levites were with much trouble collected. This shows how even a long exile had not extinguished the priestly pride in those who could no longer claim a higher rank than that of Levitical servants. When they preferred captivity to this humiliation, how can it be doubted that they considered it as a punishment from the outset, and that accordingly Ezekiel was justified in representing it as such?

So much in positive explanation of Ezekiel's statements. We do not claim to have relieved all difficulties, but may console ourselves with the thought, that even what remains dark and mysterious, stands out in a far more credible form than the absurdities to which the critical theory necessarily leads. We notice the following points: —

1. At the time of the first return from exile under Zerubbabel and Joshua, the distinction of rank between priests and Levites was so firmly established that nobody questioned its validity any longer. The whole population of Jerusalem consisted, according to 1 Chron. 9, of Israel, priests, and Levites, לְוִֹיִם כֹּהֲנִים, יִשְׂרָאֵל. On this all critics agree. But, on the critical supposition, this universal recognition of the Aaronic prerogative is a most astonishing fact. Before the exile a violent opposition was continually carried on by the provincial priests against the Zadokites at Jerusalem. No doubt, the Bamoth priests argued that the sons of Zadok possessed their exclusive rights, not *de jure*, but *de facto*. They once occupied the place, and it was impossible to expel them. This opposition continued during the first part of the exile. With the abolition of the temple-service, the Zadokites lost their only stronghold; viz., the actual occupancy of the office. From that time onward they were no more than the other Levites, like them deprived of *their* sanctuary. Instead of there being reason for the opposition to subside, and for the superiority of the sons of Zadok to gain silent recognition, all things seemed to work in the other direction. And still, a few verses of the prophet Ezekiel, in a never-realized vision, were sufficient to conjure the strife, and make out of the proud Bamoth priests, humble Levites and temple-servants! Who would believe, that from all the features in Ezekiel's vision, to which the returning exiles attached no importance, this single one was excepted, and that the slighted Levites meekly suffered the exception to their own degradation?

2. Among those who returned, there were far more priests than Levites. In the first expedition, the proportion was twelve to one. With Ezra, only thirty-eight Levites returned. How will this agree with the theory that Ezra was the writer of the Priest Code? Surely the proportion between Levites and priests there assumes a totally different character, and cannot be explained out of the actual state of affairs, immediately after the exile. Wellhausen assumes that the priesthood in Jerusalem was as numerous as that of the Bamoth. He concludes from the genealogies of the chronicler, that the proportion must have been changed in conformity with the statements of the Priest Code. This change was effected by Levitizing strange families of Nethinim, singers and janizaries. But that the Zadokites were as numerous as all the Bamoth priests together, is highly improbable; for in Ezekiel they appear as a small exception in contrast with an apostate majority. Then the assumption that non-Levitical families were Levitized rests on no historical basis whatever. And finally the critics must not only account for the proportion in Chronicles, but

for that in the Priest Code itself.

3. It is arbitrary to assume that only this part of Ezekiel's Thora had binding force, and that all other parts were utterly disregarded. If the degradation of priests to Levites was so persistently adhered to, it becomes incomprehensible how afterwards a conscientious man like Ezra could substitute a legal fiction for a divinely authorized prophecy, of which he admitted, in part at least, the obligatory character.

4. It cannot be properly called a gradual restriction, when Ezekiel limits the priesthood to the sons of Zadok, and the Priest Code confines it to the wider circle of Aaron's descendants. Thus, the Priest Code would not only have carried out one part of Ezekiel's statements, and disregarded others, but in the same matter accepted one element, and rejected the others. On Ezekiel's authority, it continues to keep down the Levites still, it goes back on the prophet's limitations, and widens the circle of favorite priests. The sons of Aaron are substituted for those of Zadok. This is no restriction, but relaxation: God's words are made of no effect. Doubtless, there had been Aaronites among the Bamoth priests. That they were afterwards re-admitted into the priesthood, *we* can understand when we recognize the ideal character of Ezekiel's prophecy; but the critics can by no means do so, who make it the basis of historical argumentation.

All this shows in what difficulties the critical theories involve us, so far as their so-called Deuteronomic period and the subsequent time are concerned. But when we go back to the pre-Deuteronomic times, the difficulties are not less numerous, and the precarious methods by which critics remove them not less obvious. We can only point out the weakest spots of the theory here, without laying claim to an exhaustive treatment of the subject.

1. The theory fails to explain how the tribe of Levi became the priestly tribe *par excellence.* A denial of this fact is impossible, since the historical testimony is too plain and unequivocal. Throughout the Old Testament, Levites appear clothed with priestly authority (Judg. 17-20, *passim;* 1 Sam. 6:15; 2 Sam. 15:24; 1 Kings 8:4, 12:31). This will never agree with a theory that holds to the original universal right of all Israelites to officiate as priests. And, apart from this, the historical basis for such a distinction as we meet here is entirely wanting in the critical scheme. The only possible solution of the mystery of Levitism is that proposed by the Priest Code, which says that God separated the tribe of Levi from the other tribes for this purpose. The historical books, moreover, testify to this origin of the distinction, 1 Sam. 2:27, 28; Deut. 33:8-11 (a so-called independent North-Israelitish document). It is easy to see how a single family could gradually form itself into an hereditary priesthood; but when, in the time of the Judges, we find a whole tribe clothed with this prerogative, we look for something more than logical possibilities in explanation. Priestly tribes do not originate in such an incidental way. If Levi possessed the priesthood in the days of the Judges, he must have possessed it long before, and obtained it at a definite point of time; since the elements out

of which a scheme of development might be constructed are entirely wanting. It seems absurd, in the face of this historical testimony, for critics to persistently deny any connection of this distinction with the facts that both Moses and Aaron were Levites, and with the momentous changes of the exodus. A historical explanation must be given here; and when one that is suitable, and accounts for all the facts, and is verified by history, presents itself, there is no ground for rejecting it. And finally, even apart from all this, the fact that from the earliest historic (according to the critics, even prehistoric) times, this distinction between Levites and non-Levites existed, is fatal to the whole hypothesis of gradual restriction. It proves, that in the history of the cultus, there was a stable and fixed element from the beginning, which, for this reason alone, cannot have arisen from unconscious development, but must have been based on intentional appointment.

It is amusing to see how the critics try to get around this fact. Wellhausen in particular makes two statements here, whose boldness, bordering upon temerity, is evidently only a cover for the weakness of his position on this important point. The first is, that no real connection whatever exists between the tribe of Levi (early dissolved into the neighboring tribes) and the priestly caste afterwards designated by that name. Both actually existed, but neither of them had any thing to do with the other. The tribe had long since disappeared when the caste rose into prominence. All this is based on a critical interpretation of Gen. 49:5-7, and clearly invented to escape the consequences which this, as we think unavoidable, combination involves. For the existence of Levi as a *priestly tribe* in the time of Judges, compare 17:7-9, 19:1, 18, and afterwards 1 Sam. 6:15, 2 Sam. 6:7.

Wellhausen's second statement is a conclusion drawn from a series of premises, which we quote from him in their logical order without any further comment, since they speak for themselves: —

(1) Jonathan the Levite, who joined the Danites, was a descendant of Moses, according to Judg. 18:30.

(2) The priestly family at Shiloh stood also in genealogical connection with Moses (!), according to 1 Sam. 2:27.

(3) There is historic probability that the house of Eli descended from Phinehas, who was, in the early period of the Judges, priest of the ark.

(4) This Phinehas, according to Josh. 24:33 (Elohistic), was a son of Eleazar.

(5) Though tradition uniformly claims Eleazar for a son of Aaron, it has no right to speak in this matter.

(6) *Eleazar* does not differ in its orthography from *Eliezer*. And *Eliezer* was a brother of Gershom, a son of Moses.

(7) When we, therefore, read Eliezer instead of Eleazar, and disregard tradition, the following facts are established: (*a*) Jonathan the Levite descended from Moses; (*b*) The priestly house at Shiloh descended from Moses.

Conclusion: All that appears of an hereditary priesthood must be explained by descent from Moses. In his family the priestly office was perpetuated. The priests at Dan and Shiloh claimed Mosaic extraction for themselves. All priests considered Moses, if not as their genealogical ancestor, still as the institutor of their guild. In Judah the guild became a "gens." Levite, at first the name of an office-bearer, now became a *nomen gentile;* and thus the Levitical priesthood originated.

2. Within the limits of the tribe of Levi itself, however, a distinction is traceable. First we have Deut. 33:8-11. The passage, as a whole, applies to the tribe of Levi (notice the transition to the plural number in ver. 9b and 10). In Moses and Aaron, Levi was proved, his fidelity tested by the Lord. But the very fact that these two were treated as representatives of the whole tribe, shows that they stood in a certain representative relation to it, not merely as leaders, but, in the case of Aaron, as the person in whom the priestly character culminated. To say the least, we have an allusion here to the peculiar position which the house of Aaron occupied in the tribe of Levi. The same representative capacity is ascribed to Aaron in the words 1 Sam. 2:27, 28.

The existence of an Aaronic priesthood is confirmed by abundant testimony, both for the beginning and the close of the period of Judges. The facts are these: (*a*) The tabernacle was in Shiloh (18:31); (*b*) It was called "*the* house of the LORD," *par excellence,* excluding, at least legally, all others (19:18); (*c*) the ark of the covenant was at Bethel (20:27); (*d*) Phinehas the son of Eleazar, the son of Aaron, "stood before it in those days." Here we have one legal sanctuary in which only the descendants of Aaron have the right to perform the highest functions, "to stand before the ark." The First Book of Samuel testifies to the same for the close of this period (1 Sam. 2:14, 22, 24, 30). Here the same indisputable facts appear, — one *universal* sanctuary served by an Aaronitic priesthood, which could only be deposed by direct divine interference, and accordingly must have been based likewise on direct divine appointment by Jehovah himself.

It has been claimed by Kuenen and others, that the passage, Deut. 33:8-11, implies the right of the whole tribe of Levi to the priestly prerogatives of bearing Urim and Thummim. But apart from the fact, that, in ver. 8, 9a the singular is used, and nothing prevents us from referring it to Aaron (or ideally to the high-priestly line descended from him), it involves no concession when we say that the "holy one" is a personification of the whole tribe. For in this case we could simply understand the passage as describing the prerogatives of the tribe, without any specification which of them belonged to the priests exclusively, which to the Levites. If it could be said that the whole tribe of Levi was proved at Massah, and striven with at the waters of Meribah, whilst only Aaron and Moses are meant, it surely is not inconsistent to say that the whole tribe had the Urim and Thummim, though in reality only the high-priest could consult them.

The name "priests" occurs thirty-four times in the books of Samuel, sixty times in those of Kings, that of Levites twice in Samuel (1 Sam. 6:15, 2 Sam.

15:24), once in Kings (1 Kings 8:4). This preponderant use of the former shows already that both terms were not synonymous. That the two offices were distinct is evident from the last reference, 1 Kings 8:4, "the priests *and* the Levites," הַכֹּהֲנִים וְהַלְוִיִּם.

That specific priestly duties are not particularly emphasized is easily accounted for when we find that in none of the numerous passages where the name occurs, was there any occasion for it (see the statement in Curtiss's "Levitical Priests," p. 89). That Levites are mentioned as handling the ark (1 Sam. 6:15) does not prove that all Levites were priests. All we can infer, is that in Beth-shemesh there were "Levitical priests." If the use of the general term "Levites" implies a denial of their descent from Aaron, we may just as well infer from the second half of the verse, that the "men of Beth-shemesh" who offered and sacrificed were not Levites. Beth-shemesh was a priestly city, so that the priests must have been present at this solemn occasion.

Of the alleged deviations in the *praxis* of that time from the Levitical law, we shall speak hereafter. A few remarks concerning the high-priest may be added. The critical opinion, that such an imposing figure as his was entirely unknown before the exile, has been stated. We must now examine the arguments adduced to sustain this statement: —

1. Wellhausen asserts, that in no product of Old Testament literature prior to the Priest Code does the term high-priest appear as a standing designation of a peculiar office, and that persons to whom the title is given are in other places called simply הַכֹּהֵן (*the priest*). Only in the Priest Code and thereafter the use of the term becomes fixed in the traditional sense. At first blush, this fact might seem to corroborate the critical theory of a gradually originating hierarchy. When examined more closely, however, it loses all value, for the following reasons: —

(*a*) The term כֹּהֵן הָרֹאשׁ (*high-priest*) appears as a synonym.

(*b*) The rare use of the name proves nothing, since it occurs only thrice in the Priest Code itself (Lev. 21:10, Num. 35:25, 28). In all other instances, the simple הַכֹּהֵן (the priest) is employed.

(*c*) The chronicler, who must have attached special importance to the name if the office was unprecedented in importance, and required historical justification, would certainly have used the term frequently. But the opposite is true. In most cases, he designates the high-priest with the simple הַכֹּהֵן (the priest). In Ezra, Joshua, the son of Jozadak, has no title at all. Neither is any found in the genealogy of the high-priests (Neh. 12:10, *seqq.*).

2. The second argument is, that no historical evidence of such an eminent position occupied by a single priest is found anywhere in the historical books. We answer, just as much there as in the Priest Code. When we leave the period of Judges out of the account, do we not find Eli, Ahijah, Ahimelech, Abiathar, Zadok, Jehoiada, Hilkiah, Azariah, all called absolutely הַכֹּהֵן, wearing the ephod, consulting the Urim and Thummim, evidently in great authori-

ty and of great influence with kings and people alike? What more can be demanded? If an explicit and accurate description of the high-priest's apparel and his work were given, how little would the critics hesitate to declare it a gloss or interpolation of later date? When assertions are made so strongly, and theories constructed so boldly, have we not the right to demand at least the evidence that somebody other than the high-priest officiated in the Holy of holies? All that can be adduced is 1 Sam. iii. 2, where Samuel is said to have slept near the ark. The passage simply means that Samuel slept within the same precincts where the ark was.

Even Wellhausen's exaggeration of the plenipotentiary authority of the high-priest after the exile, as described in the Priest Code, does not entirely lack parallels in previous times. The example of Jehoiada and the important part acted by him in the revolution that placed Joash on the throne may be remembered here. That before the exile the sanctuary was a royal dependency, is only true with reference to the apostate idolatrous Northern kingdom. While Amaziah of Bethel speaks of a king's sanctuary, מִקְדַּשׁ מֶלֶךְ, the temple at Jerusalem is, without exception, called מִקְדַּשׁ־יי, the sanctuary of Jehovah; and the priests are always כֹּהֲנֵי יי, the priests of Jehovah. Wellhausen himself admits that the Priest Code nowhere claims secular power for the high-priest. Still, in the next sentence, he does not hesitate to make the bold assertion, that beside him, no theocratic king is thinkable. If the former be true, we do not see how the latter can be maintained. Do not the historical books mention more than one instance where kings consulted their priests, and Urim and Thummim decided? And to the possibility of the co-existence of two powers, each relatively sovereign and absolute in its own sphere, the co-existence for centuries of prophetism and the kingdom abundantly testifies. The post-exilic high-priest is no more imposing figure beside Ezra and Nehemiah than Samuel beside Saul.

3. The third statement is that Deuteronomy knows nothing of a high-priest. That the blessing of Moses (xxxiii. 8-11) teaches the contrary, we have already seen (compare also xvii. 12).

Chapter Eleven - Levitical and Priestly Revenues

Closely related to the question just discussed, is that concerning Levitical and priestly revenues. The measure of priestly authority and independence must necessarily have determined the priestly income. According to Graf and Wellhausen, the following modification in the latter respect is traceable in the Codes and in the corresponding history: —

A. The priest's part of the sacrifices.

In Deuteronomy: The shoulder, the two cheeks, the maw. From the analogy of the Levites, it may be supposed that priests shared in the sacrificial meals. Originally this was the only thing which the priests could lay claim to.

In the Priest Code: Sacrificial meals become subordinate. *Minchah* (meat-offering) and *chattath* (sin-offering) and *asham* (trespass-offering) (at least in some cases) fell, as a whole, to the priest. Of *olah* (burnt-offering), the skin was for him. Of the *shelamim* (peace-offerings), the breast and the right shoulder. Wellhausen finds an approach towards *chattath* and *asham* in the fines of money mentioned in 2 Kings 12:16, "the trespass-money and sin-money."

We remark on this,— 1. The difference between the Priest Code and Deuteronomy as to sacrificial meals is entirely due to the critics imposing on the latter their self-made theory, that all sacrifices were originally nothing but sacrificial meals. There is no warrant for this in the legislation, neither do the historical books favor the view.

2. All that needs reconciliation is the apparently contradictory statement, that, according to Deuteronomy, the priests obtained the shoulder, two cheeks, and maw; according to the Priest Code of *shelamim,* the breast and the right shoulder. Here every thing will depend on our interpretation of the passage Deut. 18:3. Two opinions can be and have been actually maintained concerning it: it has been taken either as a modification of the Levitical law, or as a supplementary new legislation. The context favors the latter, which is also the traditional interpretation followed by Josephus and the Mishna and the later practice. We then understand the passage to mean, that, of all animals slaughtered for food, these three parts fell to the priest. An additional reason why we should understand the verse of private slaughtering is found in ver. 1, where the income of the priests is said to consist in "the offerings of the Lord made by fire." The word אִשֶּׁה (*fire-offering*) occurs only here in Deuteronomy, and evidently refers back to the Priest Code, where it is of extensive currency. This would involve that Deuteronomy refers to the Levitical law for a more definite statement of the priest's share, and ver. 3 becomes of necessity a new, supplementary regulation.

B. The tithes.

According to the early *praxis* (Gen. 28:22; Amos 4:4, *seqq.*) and Deuteronomy (14:22-29), the tithes are not delivered to the priests, but are carried to the sanctuary for the purpose of being eaten in sacrificial meals. Only corn, wine, and oil are tithed (ver. 23). Every third year the tithe was to be distributed among those who possessed no landed property. Wellhausen sees in the last appointment an innovation of the Deuteronomist, made in view of the destruction of the local sanctuaries.

In the Priest Code, the *clerus* lays claim to the whole tithe. At first the Deuteronomic regulations were disregarded. Afterwards a second tithe was added in conformity with the older and original *praxis.*

Another point of discrepancy is that the Priest Code extends the tithe system to cattle (Lev. 27:32), and in general to all products of husbandry. Wellhausen denies that this law was ever enforced.

1. The historical instances referred to by Wellhausen — viz., that of Jacob

and the prophecy of Amos — do not prove any thing: unless we assume the narrative in Genesis to be proleptic and unhistorical, what Jacob did will not decide what was law centuries thereafter. And Amos, in the passage referred to, does not say what was done with the tithes brought to Bethel and Gilgal. Even if we admit that a joyful meal is referred to, all may be explained by finding the so-called second tithes of Deuteronomy mentioned here. See, however, under 2.

2. The tithes in Deuteronomy do not exclude these in Leviticus, or the reverse. There is nothing inconsistent or unnatural in the assumption of two tithes, the one for the priests, the other for the offerer himself. As Wellhausen himself reminds us, Jewish tradition harmonizes the passages in this way. Or if we prefer another explanation, which indeed seems to be favored by the analogy of the first-born, it may be suggested, that the priests restored to the offerer enough of his tribute to enable him to prepare his meal. From Deuteronomy we get the impression that the cases of tithes and firstlings were of similar character. Now, it is difficult to conceive of "second first-born," so that the latter view seems to deserve the preference.

3. The very conception of *tithes* — i.e., of a definite and specified proportion of the produce — seems to involve the idea of a tribute paid to somebody. If they were destined for sacrificial meals exclusively, and had no further destination than the offerer's enjoyment, we would not expect a specification of the amount to be consumed. This consideration favors the view proposed under 2 *B*.

C. The firstlings.

Here the same principle is assumed, that all the original gifts to the Deity were destined for religious meals. When Exod. 22:30, where the first-born are commanded to be given to Jehovah, seems to contradict this assumption, Wellhausen appeals to Deuteronomy in proof that "to give to Jehovah" need not mean "to pay to the priests," but simply "to eat before Jehovah." It is significant, however, that Deuteronomy never uses the phrase "to give to Jehovah" with reference to the tithes to be eaten at the sanctuary. We are not therefore warranted to understand the passages Exod. 22:30 and Deut. 15:19 as implying nothing more than that a sacrificial meal should be eaten. That this is called "a giving to Jehovah" makes it necessary to suppose that a part, at least, fell to the priest. What is intimated in Exodus is stated in Deuteronomy; for the eating which is required in 15:20, and the sacrificing which is forbidden in ver. 21, are not synonymous, but stand in juxtaposition, so that a twofold use of the firstlings is also implied here. Thus understood, both the Covenant-law and Deuteronomy will bear out the fact, that the priest received the firstlings, but restored so much of them to the offerer as to enable him to prepare a meal. And this agrees fully with what the Priest Code teaches, Num. 18:15.

D. The Levitical cities.

Num. 35 assigns forty-eight cities to the Levites, of which thirteen fell to the priests. That the right of full possession is intended, admits of no doubt. Compare the execution of the command, Josh. 21. In addition to each city, a square of two thousand cubits was set apart, to serve for suburbs or commons.

1. The principal objection raised by critics against these appointments regards the practical impossibility of carrying them out. So first Gramberg, and afterwards Graf and Wellhausen. The latter says, "The directions to set apart a common of two thousand cubits square around the cities (in which the latter are considered as mere points), to serve as pasture-ground for the Levites, could perhaps be executed in a South-Russian steppe, or in the case of newly built cities in the West of North America, but by no means in mountainous Palestine, where such a geometrical space is nowhere to be found," etc.

2. Historical traces of the existence of these Levitical cities do not appear outside of the Book of Joshua. A considerable number of them was still in the possession of the Canaanites during the period of Judges and the early kings; e.g., Gibeon, Gezer, Taanach, Shechem.

3. In the Deuteronomic time the Levites lived scattered over all Judah: each place had its own, nowhere did they live together in a compact mass.

4. Even after the exile the situation of the Levites was not materially changed. The execution of this command was deferred until Messianic days: indeed, it did not lie within the compass of human power, and cannot have been demanded in full earnest by the Priest Code itself.

5. The first historical germs of the whole conception must be sought in the cities of asylum of Deuteronomy. All altars were originally *asyla*. But whilst the former were destroyed by Josiah's reform, of course the need of the latter remained, and was provided for by the appointment of these cities of refuge. The truth is, that all of them were priestly or Levitical cities, moreover famous seats of the old cultus. Hence the suggestion, that the law of the Priest Code arose from nothing but the reminiscences of the pre-exilic plurality of places of worship. The idea of altar and priesthood was associated with many a city, and found natural expression in declaring the forty-eight places to have been the peculiar inheritance of the *clerus* ever since the Mosaic times.

Let us briefly see what these serious charges amount to. The impracticability of the command might be considerably less than Wellhausen imagines. His objection, that the arithmetical precision with which every thing is described proves an ideal character, falls immediately away as soon as we consider the numbers given as indicating the average allowance to be made for pasture-ground, nothing more than a general limit, a minimum which might be modified according to the circumstances or the geographical condition of the country. That the cities are considered as a point is true, if we take the point, not in its geometrical sense, but as having the size of each individual city. If Wellhausen means that the square of two thousand cubits included the city, there is nothing in the text to justify this view. The comparison with newly built cities is not entirely out of place; since in the conquest of Canaan many a city must have been destroyed, and a clean sweep made. That Levitical cities remained in possession of the Canaanites is nothing remarkable, and may at the same time account for the statement of Deuteronomy and later historical facts, which presuppose a partial scattering of the Levites all over the country. Wellhausen's remark, that no traces of the existence of Levitical cities appear in subsequent time, is most positively untrue. The fact is, that some very striking coincidences make the existence of this law highly probable. We refer to what happened in Beth-shemesh; to the fact that Jeremiah, of priestly descent, was born in Anathoth; that Abiathar, when dismissed by Solomon, was told to go to Anathoth; that Nob was a residence of priests. To see in the mention of all these cities in Joshua, not the origin of their priestly character, but simply the reminiscence of it, is possible indeed; but the critics should never forget that such statements are mere applications, not proofs, of their theory. That, according to Deuteronomy, the Levites lived scattered all over the country, may be attributed to various causes. If we could grant that the critical opinion of the late origin of the book was true, the natural explanation would be, that at the schism under Jeroboam I the Levites of the Northern kingdom emigrated to Judah. This shows, however, from their own premises, that the critics have no right to conclude the non-existence of the law. But it will suffice to assume only so much prophetical foresight in Moses as enabled him to see that the Levites might not immediately or perpetually enjoy the full possession of their patrimony. For a believer in prophecy, it is not impossible to suppose that Moses, under the inspiration of God's spirit, penetrated the future, even so far as to take in the time of Jeroboam and Josiah. Deuteronomy seems to allude to the Levitical cities in chap. 18:8b: "beside that which cometh of the sale of his patrimony" (compare Keil *in loco,* from whom Schultz differs). If it must be admitted that these laws did not go into operation after the exile, what can hinder us from putting them back into the Mosaic time, and assuming that they were never fully lived up to for the same reasons that prevented their execution after the exile? As to ineffectiveness, the case stands alike; and as to historical inducements to frame such regulations, the Mosaic period certainly offered more of them than the time of Ezra. The latter must have *known* that the law was impracticable: the Israelites in the desert need not. The analogy with the cities of refuge in Deuteronomy and the division of the land in Ezekiel is so far-fetched, and there are so many discrepancies between the latter and the Priest Code, that it is impossible to assume any other real connection, than that the prophet in a free manner reproduced what was known to him from the Priest Code. That such an institution as the cities of refuge could not have taken its rise in the reign of Josiah, but must at the very least be anterior to the establishment of the kingdom, is strongly argued by Dr. A. P. Bissell, in "The Law of Asylum in Israel," Leipzig, 1884.

Chapter Twelve - Feasts

The last and most important point in regard to which the critics have attempted to point out a modification in the *praxis,* followed by a corresponding development in the laws, is that of the feasts. In the Jehovistic-Deuteronomic part of the Pentateuch, a cycle of three feasts is known (Exod. 23, 34; Deut. 16); and all these are designated by the name גח (*pilgrimage festival*): Mazzoth, *unleavened bread;* Kazir, *harvest* (Shabuoth, *weeks*); and Asiph, *ingathering* (Succoth, *tabernacles*). Whilst, with respect to the two last-mentioned, there is perfect agreement between the Jehovist and Deuteronomy, a difference appears with reference to the first. Exod. 34 connects the offering of firstlings with Mazzoth: Deuteronomy uses the name Pesach (*passover*) for the first time. The inference is, that Pesach and Mazzoth are distinct and originally independent from each other, the latter by far the elder of the two, constituting a triad with Kazir and Asiph. All three are essentially agrarian feasts. Mazzoth indicates the beginning of harvest; and accordingly a sheaf is offered to Jahveh, as the first produce of the ground in its most simple form. This is also alleged to be the original meaning of Mazzoth; viz., that of hastily prepared, inartificial bread, symbolizing the new, fresh harvest, which men do not take time carefully to leaven, to knead, and to bake (Wellhausen). Kazir closes the grain-harvest, to which the loaves of wheat bread correspond. Finally, Asiph celebrates the autumnal ingathering of oil and wine; and here the agrarian character has been preserved by dwelling in booths of branches, as is indicated by the name Succoth.

A second point, in which Deuteronomy shows an advance upon the Covenant-law, is the more definite specification of the time at which the feasts are to be held. Exod. 23 and 34 prescribe in vague and general terms, Mazzoth in the month Abib, Kazir when the wheat is cut, Asiph when the ingathering of fruits is ended. The centralization of the cultus made a more fixed date necessary, as is found in the expressions, "The first day at even," 16:4; "At even, at the going down of the sun," ver. 6; "Thou shalt turn in the morning, and go unto thy tents," ver. 7; "Seven weeks shalt thou number," ver. 9; "The feast of tabernacles seven days," ver. 13.

Thirdly, the quantity of the gifts to be brought to the feasts was at first left to the choice of the individual, afterwards settled more definitely. Exodus does not require any precise amount of the firstlings or of the produce of the field: Deuteronomy requires the tithe. In case of the first-born, of course, no determination was needed.

Fourthly, in accordance with its centralizing tendency, Deuteronomy commands that all feasts shall be kept at the sanctuary of Jehovah. On the whole, the primitive cycle of feasts is said to have a purely agricultural basis: it is only in Deuteronomy that the first modest traces may be seen of that substituting history for nature, of which the later legislation is so fruitful.

The peculiarities and innovations of the Priest Code are by Wellhausen stated under the following heads: —

1. The sacrificial meals of the feasts have given place to minutely pre-scribed burnt- and sin-offerings (Num. 28).

2. The aparchae (*first-fruits* and *firstlings*) are separated from the feasts: they appear no longer as offerings, but have been transformed into priestly revenues.

3. The date of the harvest-feasts is now definitely settled, — Mazzoth on the fifteenth of the first month, Succoth on the fifteenth of the seventh month, Shabuoth seven weeks after Mazzoth. This shows that they have ceased to be purely agrarian feasts, which, as such, could never have been bound to a fixed date, but were dependent on the ripeness of the harvest.

4. The historical interpretation of the feasts is carried to the extreme. Suc-coth becomes a memorial of the dwelling in tents in the desert. Passover is not merely made a sacrament, but a sort of mass: it was celebrated, accord-ing to the Priest Code, in the night of the exodus, and effected the salvation of Israel. In the same manner, the keeping of Mazzoth is already commanded before the exodus. Only on Shabuoth no historical interpretation is imposed.

5. The Priest Code requires that all feasts from beginning to end shall be kept at Jerusalem, and in this respect advances upon Deuteronomy. For by requiring a Mikra Kodesh (holy convocation) on the seventh day of Mazzoth, visitors who did not live in the immediate neighborhood of Jerusalem were under the necessity of remaining there through the whole feast-week. To Succoth the Priest Code adds an eighth day. In Ezekiel, both Mazzoth and Succoth are still limited to seven days each (chap. 45).

6. The Priest Code has added two new feasts to the original cycle of three; viz., the feast of Teruah (trumpets), on the first of the seventh month, and the Yom Kippurim (Day of Atonement), on the tenth of the same month. During the exile the ecclesiastical new year began on the tenth of the seventh month. The Day of Atonement was not observed before the year 444 B.C., or even later, and had its origin in the commemoration of the days of Jerusalem's de-struction during the exile by fasting. Ezekiel mentions two days of reconcilia-tion, the one falling on the new moon of the seventh month (45:20, according to the Septuagint). Afterwards the Priest Code reversed the order of the new year and Kippurim by putting the latter on the tenth, and the former on the first, day of the seventh month.

7. The law of the Sabbath-year is modified by the Priest Code in two par-ticulars (*a*) What was a relative year in Exod. 23:10, 11, is now absolutely fixed; *all* fields have to rest in the same year. (*b*) Not only reaping, but also sowing, is to be suspended. The Year of Jubilee is entirely an invention of the Priest Code.

The first attempt to establish the theory just stated, occupies itself with pointing out the naturalistic origin of the triad of main feasts. Wellhausen takes great pains to claim for all of them a purely agricultural basis. The πρῶτον ψεῦδς of his reasoning consists in the assumption that this natural-istic basis would exclude an additional historical sanction or confirmation.

We grant that its relation to the harvest was probably the only significance of Pentecost, and admit that such a relation exists with regard to Mazzoth and Succoth, but do not bind ourselves by this concession to the naturalistic denial of all other accessary historical associations.

More than this. We maintain that the imposition of this theory, on what the critics claim to be the earliest legislation and the earliest history, cannot be accomplished without the most arbitrary methods of reconstructing history and of misinterpreting Scripture. This admits of demonstration in detail. We hope to show that the historical origin of the feasts, in addition to their natural basis, is not only possible, but absolutely required by all accessible evidence. What falls outside of this, is, of course, pure hypothesis.

Let us examine the primitive laws. For Pentecost, a historical basis is nowhere claimed. For Succoth, only in the Priest Code (Lev. 23:43). For Mazzoth and Pesach (Passover), however, in *all* the laws *without a single exception:* both are *always* brought in connection with the exodus (Exod. 23, 34; Deut. 16). This fact is a serious obstacle in the way of Wellhausen's naturalizing presentations. It is wonderful how innocently he tries to remove it, as if a mere incidental feature, and not a vital principle, were at stake. He remarks that the cycle presupposes the original similarity of all its members. Hence, if Kazir and Asiph are harvest-feasts, Mazzoth *cannot* have been a historical one. This critical *"cannot"* is weighty enough in Wellhausen's view to set aside the explicit testimony of both the Covenant-law and Deuteronomy. A semblance, indeed, of proof is adduced: "The feast proper is not called Hag-ha-Pesach, but Hag-ha-Mazzoth: only the latter stands co-ordinate with both the other harvest-feasts...For a companion with Kazir and Asiph, only Mazzoth can come under consideration."

It is difficult to see what is gained by this violent separation of Mazzoth from Pesach. But let us suppose for a moment that the two could be severed. Would this alter the case with regard to Mazzoth? Not in the least; for in the Covenant-law the exodus is twice mentioned as the historical ground of *Mazzoth, and not of Pesach.* Wellhausen's language conveys the erroneous impression that the primitive laws brought only Pesach in connection with the exodus. The opposite is true: the passages in Exod. 23 and 34 do not so much as mention Pesach; and in Deuteronomy, though Pesach is made more prominent than Mazzoth, still the great fact of deliverance from Egypt is almost exclusively combined with the latter.

Let us now consider in how far the severance of Pesach and Mazzoth can be justified. In Exod. 23:15 no allusion to the Passover appears. But in ver. 18 it is said, "Thou shalt not offer the blood of my sacrifice with leavened bread; neither shall the fat of my sacrifice remain until the morning." We do not know how Wellhausen understands this verse, but to us every other explanation but that which refers it to the Passover-lamb seems unnatural: ver. 18 is evidently an appendix to ver. 15 (Mazzoth), ver. 19a to ver. 16 (Kazir), ver. 19b to ver. 16b (Asiph). So Hengstenberg, Bertheau, Knobel, Bachmann, Keil.

The passage 34:25 is parallel. Moreover, in Exod. 34:19, 20, the command to give the male first-born of men and animals to Jehovah is immediately subjoined to the Mazzoth-law. The offering of the first-born belongs to Pesach, so that also in this passage the two appear inseparably connected. Deuteronomy makes Mazzoth already subordinate to Pesach. So they must have coexisted already for a considerable time, and not only this, but have been intimately connected.

We take it to be established beyond doubt, that, according to the Covenant-law and Deuteronomy, the institution of Mazzoth rested on a divine act of deliverance that, though in part an agricultural feast, it had at the same time a national and historic character. If, however, Pesach is so closely allied to Mazzoth, that the two always appear together, it would seem fair to infer the historical basis of the latter from that of the former.

On the other hand, the question of Pesach is one of the most intricate and difficult problems which the newer criticism will have to solve. The numerous hypotheses proposed in explanation of this mystery may help us to form an estimate of the hopelessness of the task. We cannot enter into a discussion of all these, for the simple reason, that none of them rests on either exegetical or historical warrant, or even claims to rest on such; they are hypotheses in the true sense of the word, products of the critical imagination: and we shall confine ourselves to scriptural facts.

The name even is not clear. No satisfactory etymology, besides the scriptural one, has as yet been given. Wellhausen says, "Essentially Pesach is the feast of the offering of the first-born." The natural inference would seem to be, that this definition confirms our view of the historical origin of the feast. For the right of Jehovah to Israel's first-born is, so far as we know, everywhere founded on his sparing them when he slew the first-born of the Egyptians. This is not only the case in the Priest Code, but also in the Jehovist (Exod. 13:11, *seqq*.). Wellhausen is candid enough to admit this. How, then, does he avoid the inference fatal to his theory? His first recourse is to the dissecting-knife of analytical criticism. He declares that (also on other grounds) the whole section (13:1-16) does not belong to the sources of the Jehovist, but was added by a Deuteronomic redactor. We cannot follow him into this labyrinth of divisive operations. But let us suppose that the passage be Deuteronomic. It is in any case, together with Deut. 16, according to Wellhausen's own view, the first explicit statement concerning Pesach. As such, it has the right to be heard as the oldest historical testimony accessible. That the critics refuse to recognize the historic credibility of Deuteronomy, we cannot help. Still, a reason must be given why the Deuteronomist, seeking an historical ground for the origin of Pesach, hit exactly upon this point, Israel's exodus from Egypt.

Wellhausen helps himself by the following hypothesis: The exodus occurred, according to early tradition, about the time of the ancient spring-festival. Exod. 5:1, Moses and Aaron ask from Pharaoh, "Let my people go, that they may hold a feast unto me in the wilderness." This is made to prove that the feast existed before the historical occasion assigned to it in the law. Also chap. 12 ver. 21 is quoted, where Moses addresses the elders of Israel with the words, "Kill *the* Passover." The feast was the occasion of the exodus. Afterwards the order was reversed; and after the feast had thus been supplied with an historical basis, its main and original feature, the offering of the first-born, required an explanation also. This was found in the narrative of God's slaying the first-born of Egypt. And he adds, "Unless we assume the existence of the custom to offer the firstborn, the narrative becomes unexplainable and no reason is given why the pestilence made such a strange selection."

That this is unscrupulously distorting facts to suit a theory, the critic seems not to feel. Not a particle of evidence, either in law or in history, can be claimed to favor this hypothesis. That it is the only thing "which suits the nature of the case," is true, if the transactions were purely natural. This is exactly what we deny, the very point at issue: to assume it, is openly begging the question. To those who believe in the supernatural element in history, it may be somewhat easier than for Wellhausen to explain why the pestilence made such a strange selection among the Egyptians.

The two passages quoted from Exodus decide nothing. Exod. 5:1 only proves that the Israelites desired to keep *a* feast. That it was an annually recurring feast, is not stated, and rather doubtful. But if we grant that a spring-festival was observed, this cannot warrant Wellhausen in discarding all additional historical explanation. That Moses said to the elders, "Kill the Passover," is due to the writer unconsciously putting a term familiar to himself into the mouth of the speaker. Of course, the narrative does not pretend to give the *ipsissima verba* of Moses' communication to the elders.

After all, the former of these passages would make strongly against Wellhausen's theory of Mazzoth being an agricultural feast. The Israelites desired to hold a festival in the desert. And a rural festival in the wilderness is a downright absurdity. How impossible it is to put Mazzoth on a par with Kazir and Asiph, is seen from two other features: (*a*) Mazzoth occupied seven days, Kazir only one: had both been rural festivals, the one to celebrate the beginning, the other the completion, of harvest, we would expect the latter to have lasted the longer. (*b*) Wellhausen's explanation touching the origin of eating unleavened bread, leaves out of view that *all leaven bread had to be removed out of the houses*. How this feature will ever be explained on naturalistic principles, it is not easy to determine.

Another consideration would be enough to disprove the naturalistic element, which all newer hypotheses with regard to Pesach have in common; viz., that it was simply a sacrificial feast, on which the first-born, either in reality or by substitution, were offered to God. We refer to the fact, that, in connection with it, the male first-born of *men* are claimed for Jehovah. If the offering of the firstborn was the occasion of a spring-feast, and this the origin of Pesach, we must logically infer that at this spring-festival also human sacrifices were brought. The two commands stand on a par, and logic is severe. It is impossible to see how the idea of offering human first-born could ever arise in connection with Pesach, at so early a time that the Jehovist already combines the two, unless they were actually combined. We must, then, assume that this primitive prehistoric rural feast witnessed the terrible scenes of manslaughter in honor of the Deity. In spite of all his naturalism, Wellhausen is not inclined to follow others, who actually hold that human sacrifices were more or less common among the Israelites. He is candid enough to admit, that only a few examples of such a horrible practice are found, and that it appears as throughout voluntary and exceptional. Not until shortly before the exile did the burning of children become more customary.

It must be necessary to account for the combination in some other way. We look for this in vain. All that Wellhausen gives us is contained in this sentence: "When the human first-born are also claimed, this is nothing but a later generalization. It will not escape the thoughtful reader, that *this* is nothing but a groundless assertion. And, at any rate, the generalization needs an explanation just as much as the practice.

Under these circumstances, where all the evidence is on our side, and on the other hand the critics are obliged to support one assumption by another, we must protest against all naturalistic explanations of Pesach which make any higher pretensions than that of being logically possible. The old historical view, given by the Bible in Exod. 12, accounts fully for all the facts, gives a plausible etymology of the name, is not half so one-sided as that of the critics, since it does not exclude the connection between Passover and the incipient harvest. That neither the Covenant-law nor Deuteronomy alludes to the historical associations of Succoth, cannot be made to speak for a later origin of this historical idea. Even in the Priest Code these historical associations are not made prominent. The whole tenor of the law, Lev. 23:39-43, shows that the main end of the feast was to celebrate the autumnal ingathering of fruit. The customary dwelling in booths in memory of the desert-journey was secondary, and is only incidentally referred to at the end in a single verse. And here also it appears what the *argumentum e silentio* is worth. The remarkable fact is, that both the Jehovist and Deuteronomist place Pesach or Mazzoth in a historical light; the Priest Code, on the contrary, does not so much as allude to its historical character in Lev. 23, — in both cases, exactly the opposite of what the critical theory would lead us to expect. Surely, no critic would infer from this silence that the agricultural significance of Mazzoth was unknown to the Jehovist and the Deuteronomist. Just as little need we infer from their silence as to the historical character of Succoth, that this must have been the fruit of a later development.

We turn to Deuteronomy, and ask in what the pretended advance upon the Covenant-law consists. The dates of the feasts are said to have been more definitely fixed, in accordance with the centralization of the cultus. The truth is, that no dates are given besides a single relative one; viz., that Shabuoth shall be seven weeks from Pesach. But this is no advance, nor is the specification new in Deuteronomy; since Exod. 34 already uses the name Shabuoth, which implies the dependence of the feast for its computation upon Mazzoth. All the other specifications of time regard only the duration of the feast, or the exact time of day to begin its observance, all which cannot have had any thing to do with the centralization of the cultus. On the contrary, where a specification for this purpose might be expected, it is not made. Chap. 16:1, "Observe the month of Abib," is even more indefinite than the Jehovistic phrase, "in the time appointed of the month Abib," Exod. 23:15. Indeed, it is hardly conceivable, if Deuteronomy was written with the tendency ascribed to it by the critics, that the author would have failed to secure what was first of all necessary to centralization; viz., to fix for each feast a definite date.

Deuteronomy, it is alleged, shows an advance by defining the exact quantity of the produce of the field which had to be brought to the feasts. It does not appear, however, that Deuteronomy identifies the first-fruits and the tithes in this way. They were distinct, and are kept so in chap. 26, where ver. 1-11 treat of the first-fruits, ver. 12-15 of the third year's tithe. Naturally the first-fruits, the quantity of which is nowhere determined (chap. 26, a basket), would be taken along at the occasion of a feast still, this is nowhere prescribed. The command to give the first-born to Jehovah is in Exod. 34:19 subjoined to that of Mazzoth on account of the historical connection. Chap. 22:30 seems even to preclude the offering at a feast; as it says, "The eighth day thou shalt give it me." Exod. 23:19 refers probably to the single sheaf of Shabuoth. The only evidence in favor of this view lies in the position of Deut. 15:19-23 immediately before the Passover-law. Indeed, when we combine this with the injunction to sacrifice the Passover to the Lord of the flock and the herd, the suggestion gains in plausibility that the firstlings were offered at Passover or Mazzoth. But this is far from proving Wellhausen's theory, that the feasts were originally nothing else than occasions to offer the *aparchae*. The law knows nothing of such an identification of the two, any more than it identifies tithes and first-fruits. An explicit statement would in both cases have been necessary, as Wellhausen himself admits. "In the Jehovistic and Deuteronomic Codes, the connection between *aparchae* and feasts is rather assumed than expressed." And assumed it is, not, however, by the laws, but by the critic himself.

With regard to the four peculiarities of the Priest Code first mentioned, little need be said. That sacrificial meals were changed into minutely defined sin- and burnt-offerings, rests on the utterly fallacious notion, that, until shortly before the exile, all sacrifices were sacrificial meals. We have spoken of this before. It is self-evident that the feast-offerings of the Priest Code (Num. 28) do not exclude וּבָקָר צֹאן (*flock and herd*), which Deuteronomy commands to be freely offered, and then to be eaten before the LORD. The whole passage in Deuteronomy does not purport to give complete regulations concerning the feasts and their ceremonies and sacrifices, but simply considers them under the one great aspect, that of unity of cultus, for the maintenance of which they were one of the most effectual and important means.

The *aparchae*, it is further alleged, are separated from the feasts: they appear no longer as offerings, but have been transformed into priestly revenues. We have already seen that Deut. 15:19-23 furnishes the only support to the view that the *aparchae* were connected with the feasts at all. Historical probability is all that can be claimed here. But that the Priest Code severs the *aparchae* from the feasts is positively untrue. It simply does not specify a time when they shall be offered, and this for the obvious reason, that the words, Num. 18, are addressed to the priests, who were the receivers, and not to the people. The other half of Wellhausen's statement is equally inaccurate. It is true that the Priest Code makes the *aparchae* priestly revenues. Compare Num. 18:13, 15. Still, the context itself shows that this is not meant in such a sense as would be inconsistent with the evident purpose indicated in Deut. 14 and 15, that they should serve as a joyful meal to the offerer. Num. 18:17, 18, shows that the first-born were to be offered as *shelamim*, with this distinction only, that not only breast and shoulder, but all the flesh, fell to the priests. Now, when we remember that probably all the first-born came in at the same time of Passover, it becomes almost impossible that the priests should have kept all this to themselves. The most natural inference is, that they restored a portion of the meat to the offerer, sufficiently large to enable him to keep the meal mentioned in Deuteronomy.

Thirdly, the critics discover an advance in the fact that the Priest Code has finally settled the dates of all the feasts. The main point is, to show that the original conception of agricultural feasts has been entirely lost. The latter, depending on the ripeness of the harvest, cannot be bound to any definite date.

The critics must admit that the Priest Code does not only recognize an agricultural element in its feast-laws, but dwells upon it with special emphasis in the case of both Mazzoth and Succoth (Lev. 23). Still, it assigns to each a fixed date. Is any thing more required to show that both are perfectly consistent, and that the law could definitely appoint the time of observance without giving the skeptical critics any well-grounded suspicion that the two could not go together? How impracticable that Priest Code must have been!

But in the fourth place, still graver charges are made against it. It is accused of fictitiously substituting historical combinations for the natural basis of the feasts. We saw how little this is the case. Lev. 23 does not mention the historical occasion of the institution of Pesach and Mazzoth, whereas both the Jehovist and the Deuteronomist do so. Also in the case of Succoth, the historical element is given only a secondary importance. Succoth is the only feast for whose historical significance we have independent testimony outside of the law in Hos. 12:10.

That in Exod. 12, Pesach and Mazzoth are instituted not merely in commemoration of the exodus, but as an effectual means of saving Israel, is true. The cause, however, lies not in any tendency pursued by the author, but in the peculiar position of Israel. Their whole history, and relation to the Gentiles, were typical of the relation of God's saved people to the world. Hence, that which distinguished them from the Egyptians, and secured their safety from the slaying angel, could be nothing else than a type of that great Passover-lamb, participation in which would one day distinguish the spiritual Israel from the world under condemnation. The case finds a parallel in the institution of our Lord's supper before the crucifixion.

By prescribing a Mikra Kodesh (holy convocation) on the seventh day of Mazzoth, the Priest Code makes it obligatory for all Israelites to spend the whole feast in Jerusalem. Critics find in this a new advance upon Deuteronomy. Stähelin, Von Lengerke, De Wette, Hupfeld, and Knobel understand by Mikra Kodesh a holy convocation at the central sanctuary, so that a pilgrimage thither was required.

Though the words in themselves might have this meaning, the view becomes untenable when we see that a Mikra Kodesh was appointed not less than three times for one — viz., the seventh — month. Since it would have been impossible to demand three pilgrimages to Jerusalem in one month, the phrase must necessarily denote any convocation in a local place of worship, for the purpose of observing the day. Hence we reach the conclusion, that neither in Leviticus nor in Deuteronomy does the law determine how long the Israelites were to remain at the sanctuary at the annual feasts. That the prevalent custom was to stay all seven days, is probable. Still, the law does not expressly demand it. Deut. 16:7 seems even to indicate the contrary: "Thou shalt turn in the morning, and go unto thy tents." As they suppose that the laws require a seven days' stay, Keil and Riehm take this as signifying a return to their homes and lodgings at the place of the sanctuary. This involves the assumption, that the Passover was eaten in the court of the sanctuary by all Israelites, which would have been hardly practicable. We understand ver. 7 as containing a permission to return after the first night. That the custom was to remain during the whole feast, is not denied. But the law allowing this return in the morning, evidently tries to emphasize the absolute necessity of being at the place of the sanctuary at least during that one night. To both Mazzoth and Succoth, the Priest Code adds one day, according to Wellhausen. That Lev. 23 assigns eight days to Succoth is clear. On the other hand, Deuteronomy speaks only of seven days of the feast. Its silence respecting the eighth day עֲצֶרֶת (solemn assembly) is easily accounted for. The purpose of Deuteronomy was not to lay down minute rules for feast-observance. So only the feast proper, consisting of seven days, is summarily referred to. And even the Priest Code does not consider the eighth day as an essential part of the feast. It is rather a close to the whole cycle of feasts, and consequently added to the last. Num. 29:35, in assigning to it fewer sacrifices than to the feast proper, puts this beyond doubt. The notion that the Priest Code makes Mazzoth one day longer than Deuteronomy, arises simply from the popular use of the date in Lev. 23:5, "On the fourteenth day of the first month at eve," evidently meaning, "On the evening with which the fifteenth day begins." This was also the beginning of the first Mazzoth-day, and so no contradiction exists.

We come now to the last and most serious charge against the Priest Code viz., that it has added two new feasts, unknown before, that of Teruah (trumpets) and the Yom Kippurim (Day of Atonement). That the Priest Code adds new feasts, is inaccurate. Lev. 23 does not enumerate the feasts, but simply the Moedim (appointed seasons) on which a Mikra Kodesh (holy convocation) was held. That neither the Covenant-law nor Deuteronomy makes mention of these two Moedim, is in consequence of their enumerating only such feasts as required an appearance before the LORD at the sanctuary. Hence the Sabbath is not even alluded to in connection with the feast-laws. Since Teruah and Yom Kippurim required only a Mikra Kodesh, they are omitted.

In so far as Wellhausen holds that before the exile the Jewish year began in the autumn, it is strange that he should consider Teruah as of post-exilic origin. It is highly probable *a priori,* that the beginning of the harvest-year was celebrated by a feast, the more so since the ordinary observance of the new moons would naturally lead to it. But this point also must be utilized to prove the late origin of the Priest Code. During the exile, the Jews derived their spring-era from the Babylonians, whose year, according to Assyriologists, began in the spring. The Priest Code wishing to preserve the old autumn-year, made a distinction between the civil and the ecclesiastical year. Against this hypothesis of Wellhausen, the simple reference to such passages as 2 Sam. 11:1; 1 Kings 20:22, 26; Jer. 36:9, 22, and *passim,* may suffice. For the rest, even Graf admits (p. 40), that, from the silence of the previous Codes, no conclusion as to the non-existence of Teruah can be drawn.

The argument against a pre-exilic existence of the Day of Atonement is twofold. First, the common *argumentum e silentio.* Little need be said about this. The critics agree that the cycle of the three great feasts dates back to the earliest times of the possession of Canaan. Instead of repeated mention, as we would expect, we find the observance of Shabuoth but once stated before the exile (2 Chron. 8:13), Succoth four times (probably Judg. 21:19 and 1 Sam. 1:20, 21; 1 Kings 8:2, 12:32), Pesach twice (probably Isa. 30:29; 2 Kings 23:21), the three together (1 Kings 9:25 and 2 Chron. 8:13). At the same time the prophets speak in terms which presuppose a fixed cycle of yearly feasts (Isa. 29:1). When we add to this, that the *argumentum e silentio,* strictly applied, would bring the origin of the Day of Atonement down to the time of John Hyrcanus, or even of Herod the Great (37 B.C.), little more need be added.

In Ezek. 40:1, we read that the prophet received his vision in "the beginning of the year, in the tenth day of the month." Ezekiel follows the autumn-era in other instances (compare chap. 45:18, 20). Accordingly, Lev. 25:9

would be parallel, where the Year of Jubilee is said to begin on the tenth day of the seventh month, in the Day of Atonement. As the critics recognize a close relationship between Lev. 18-26 and Ezekiel, the inference would not be rash, that Ezekiel takes "the beginning of the year" and "the tenth day of the month" as synonymous; was acquainted with the Year of Jubilee as beginning on that particular day, and consequently with the Day of Atonement itself, since its connection with the beginning of the year of release was not incidental, but of deep significance (compare Isa. 58, especially ver. 5). Wellhausen avoids the inference by declaring בְּיוֹם הַכִּפֻּרִים (*in the Day of Atonement*) an interpolation of a later hand, and is consequently obliged to assume that to Ezekiel the new year began on the 10th of Tisri. How this happened to fall on the tenth of a month, he does not explain; for what is said on p. 114 hardly deserves the name of an explanation. That it became easy, after the beginning of the civil year had been transferred to spring, to fix upon any date whatever, is not true. The old date, Tisri 1, was there; and what could have occasioned its change from the beginning to the middle of the month, it is not easy to see.

But there is another way of arguing *e silentio*. It is alleged that there are certain pre-exilic passages, where mention of the day would have been appropriate, or even necessary, had it been in existence. We give them in their order of occurrence, and add a few explanatory remarks to each respectively:

[1] — In 1 Kings 8:68, the consecration of the temple is said to have occasioned a double feast. The feast referred to in ver. 2 must have been Succoth. The chronicler gives his comment upon this in his second book (7:7-10). According to him, the last seven days closed on the twenty-third of the seventh month. Hence the additional seven days preceded the common Succoth-week. But then they extended from the eighth of the month onward, and the feast of consecrating the temple coincided with the Day of Atonement. Since the latter was a day of affliction, this would have been impossible and critics claim to have here the most conclusive argument, that no Day of Atonement existed either in Solomon's time or in that of the chronicler. For the chronicler would not have failed to notice and correct the incongruity, had it really existed. We remark,—

1. The conception of the Day of Atonement was not so much that of sadness and gloom, as to be entirely inconsistent with the consecration of the temple (compare Isa. 58). Both the Mishna and Gemara present it as a day of joy.

2. If the consecration of the temple was going on, and no rites and ceremonies could be legally performed before this came to an end, it was not strange if the observance of the Day of Atonement was disregarded for once. The idea of purifying a sanctuary newly built, not yet quite consecrated, and filled with the glorious presence of God, is absurd.

3. That, according to the chronicler, Solomon put this initiatory feast at the time of the yearly atonement, is highly significant, and contained rather an allusion to the day than a proof of its non-existence.

Ezra 3:1-6. From Tisri 536 the full sacrificial service commenced. Accordingly, neither Yom Teruah nor Yom Kippurim was observed. But how could the latter, when, according to ver. 6b, the foundation of the temple of the LORD had not yet been laid?

In Neh. 8:13-17, which speaks of the year B.C. 444, the feast of tabernacles is observed, but as something new. This shows, says Wellhausen, that the Thora, which contained Lev. 23 (with the exception of ver. 26-32), had not yet been promulgated, and was now published by Ezra and Nehemiah in this very year 444.

From Ezra 3:4, it is clear that an absolute ignorance of Succoth cannot be assumed. The emphasis in the passage referred to, lies evidently in the so (8:17). Hence the theory, that Ezra now published the Code for the first time, finds no support in this fact; and no inference of the non-existence of the Day of Atonement can be drawn. Compare, for a parallel case, Deut.23:4-6 with Neh. 13:1. The fast-day in Neh. 9 is radically different in conception from the Day of Atonement.

Ezekiel mentions no Day of Atonement, but only two days of reconciliation, on the first of the first and seventh month respectively. Apart from the fact that Ezekiel is also silent with regard to other feasts, of which we know he was not ignorant (e.g., Shabuoth), we have seen already that chap. 40:1 contains probably an allusion to this day. And it is far more probable, that the two days of reconciliation were a modification of the Day of Atonement than the reverse.

Even the post-exilic Zechariah is summoned as a witness against this day. Graf says, "When interrogated concerning the commemorative fast-days, he does not even allude to the Day of Atonement" (chap 7 and 8). The simple reason is, that he had no occasion to do so. For the Day of Atonement was not a day of sad historical remembrance, not a "*dies ater*" in the sense in which the four referred to were.

There are several considerations which make the high antiquity of this day very plausible.

1. All ancient peoples had special feasts of purification. It is not likely that the Israelites formed an exception.

2. It is difficult to conceive how, without any precedent in the practice before the exile, such a fiction could, after the exile, have found immediate acceptance.

3. That the Day of Atonement was not so universally observed, and did not make such a deep impression upon the national life of the people, must be attributed to its deep spiritual significance. The joyful agricultural feasts appealed more to the national inclinations than the day of affliction to the consciousness of sin.

4. That, especially after the exile, more traces of such a consciousness appear, must be explained on the same ground. The judgment of the captivity

had greatly deepened the sense of sin, and taught them better to appreciate this atoning feast.

5. The ceremony with the goat for Azazel points to a high antiquity. So also other forms of language.

6. The most incredible feature of the newer theory is, that at a time when no ark or mercy-seat existed any longer, or could be hoped ever to exist again, the law should have been framed in which they play such a prominent, almost exclusive, part.

7. The critics cannot help themselves by merely removing Lev. 16 from the Priest Code. The whole Code in all its parts abounds in references to it (compare Exod. 30:10, Lev. 23, 25). Num. 8:7 is very striking. Also the name of the mercy-seat, כַּפֹּרֶת reminds us of the solemn ceremony of sprinkling atoning blood on the cover of the ark once a year.

Finally, Wellhausen asserts that the Priest Code makes of the relative Sabbath-year an absolute one, which required all fields to rest at the same time. But the expressions in Exod. 23:10, 11, do not decide either for or against Wellhausen's theory, that at first the year was chosen arbitrarily by each individual for each separate field. And his second statement, that the Priest Code advances upon the Covenant-law by requiring the suspension of sowing also, rests on a mistaken exegesis of Exod. 23:11, which refers the suffix (it), not אֶרֶץ (land), but תְּבוּאָה (fruit), of the preceding verse. That the Year of Jubilee does not appear in any previous legislation, need not awake surprise. Neither does the Covenant-law mention new moons. It is true, history offers no instance in which the law was observed; but this simply shows that it was in a certain sense very *impracticable*, and difficult to carry out. Still, the prophets allude to it (compare Isa. 58, 61:1; Ezek. 46:17).

We have reached the end of our discussion of the pretended development in the cultus of Israel. However deficient it may have been, we hope it shows that the newest Pentateuchal criticism has weak points in its very strongholds. No single point has been discovered which was utterly inconsistent with the unity of the Codes. We approach a new topic now. Having found the unity of the laws in Exodus-Numbers confirmed by positive proof, and the objections brought against it unfounded, we may proceed to consider the relation of this body of the law to Deuteronomy.

[1] For much on this point, we are indebted to the paper of Dr. Delitzsch in Luthardt's Zeitschrift, 1880, Heft. iv.

Chapter Thirteen - Unity of Deuteronomy and the Laws of the Intermediate Books

On the essential unity of Deut. 5-26, all critics agree. They differ somewhat in opinion as to the subsequent parts of the book. Also, the introductory chapters have been severed from the bulk of the book, which is legal. Still, they are often attributed to the same author, who forged the Code, and composed them afterwards to unite his book with the Jehovistic document. For example, Graf holds that Jeremiah was the author of Deut. 1-30. Kayser ascribes to one and the same author, 4:44-26, 27 in part, and 28. He does not decide whether the introductory and closing chapters belong to him or not (p. 141). Kuenen thinks that chap. 1:1-32:47 were composed as one piece.

When we speak here of unity, it is obviously in a wider sense than before. The Sinaitic legislation was given within a few months, whilst between it and Deuteronomy fall more than forty years. It is not unity of time, much less of circumstances and environment, but unity of authorship of spirit and aim, and of underlying ideas, which we seek. Even the old view of Delitzsch, who held that a man like Joshua, or one of the elders, זְקֵנִים, on whom the spirit of Moses rested, supplemented the Elohistic narrative by writing Deuteronomy, maintains the essential unity in this wide sense. Kleinert's view, on the other hand, that Deuteronomy was written in the time of Samuel, would already give it up; and to speak of laws, originating in as late a period as that of the Kings, as Mosaic, is not only inaccurate, but misleading.

We are chiefly concerned with two questions here: —
1. Does a relative unity between Deuteronomy and the middle books exist?
2. To which of the two must we assign the priority?

1. Does a relative unity exist?
The peculiar character of Deuteronomy has been defined in various ways, owing to the fact that individual traits have been exclusively emphasized, and made to account for all the others. Kurtz and Riehm describe it as the people's Code, and find in this destination the main distinction from the Levitical legislation. Keil speaks of "a hortatory description, explanation, and enforcement of the most essential contents of the Covenant relation and Covenant-laws, with emphatic prominence given to the spiritual principle of the law and its fulfillment." Ewald as "a fresh and independent law, standing side by side with the earlier one, — a transformation of the old law, to suit altered circumstances." Schultz gives as the aim of the book, "to secure by supplementary regulations that the laws and institutions of the previous books, whose full validity is presupposed, shall be observed, not only in an external way, but as to their inner significance, their higher aim, their spiritual principle, etc.

A comparison of all these definitions will be the best test of their accuracy. Once admitted that each of them has some support in the book, their deficiency will immediately appear by observing that they do not cover each other. That Deuteronomy is the people's Code, does not explain why it should not only interpret, but also enlarge and add. The same objection may be raised against Schultz's definition and that of Keil. The supplementary character of the Code is by no means so accidental and secondary that it can be overlooked in a definition.

Another inference is, how little right we have to determine the date of a book from the indications of a single feature. All these traits must have an underlying common cause. Their bearing upon the critical question of authenticity can be truly estimated only when this deeper principle has been recognized. Individual features derive their true significance from their common source, and severed from this are very likely to be misinterpreted.

This one principal tendency seems to have been best appreciated by Hävernick. He recognizes two prominent contrasts with the Levitical law, — *subjectivity* and *parenesis* or hortatory character. Proceeding on this observation, Hävernick finds in Deuteronomy the fundamental type of all Old-Testament prophecy. "Moses appears here as a prophet, נָבִיא; and subsequent prophetism is considered as nothing but the development of his work, standing with it in the most intimate and vital connection."

It is remarkable how much light is shed by a just appreciation of this principle on all other features of the Code. That it addresses the people, no longer awakens surprise. Prophecy roots itself in the law, not abolishing, counteracting, or modifying it, but explaining, exhorting, enforcing, above all things evolving the spiritual kernel from the objective external form. Subjectivity and a reflective character are adequately explained. Once more, prophecy does not indulge in scholastic repetition of separate statutes, but seizes upon the prominent points, which, under the circumstances of the time, need special elucidation and enforcement. Thus also for what the Code passes by in silence, Hävernick's view assigns a satisfactory ground of omission. How it embraces the features which Schultz has so well brought out, is self-evident. Not less does it include the view of Ewald and Riehm, for Moses is prophet and legislator at the same time. Hävernick says, "As mediator of the Old Covenant, he stands at the summit of all prophecy: ...the distinctive character of his work is, that it not merely approaches the law from the stand-point of subjective application, but also develops and completes it."

The correctness of this view may further be tested by its applicability to all the phenomena. We cannot enter upon the matter in detail, but only indicate the rough outlines along which the argument ought to proceed.

(1) Instead of God speaking to Moses, and Moses to Aaron and his sons, Moses speaks here directly as God's mouthpiece in long discourses to the people. That such is the conception of prophecy, the book states itself (18:15, *seqq.*).

(2) The hortatory, parenetical style exhibits a mind not bound by the letter of the law, but aroused and swayed by the powerful impulse of direct inspiration.

(3) The generalizing method, which seizes upon points of present practical importance, adapts and applies the law to the wants of contemporary history, and emphasizes principles instead of giving legal *minutiae,* exhibits a striking conformity to the work of the later prophets.

(4) The generic treatment of the future. Where there is foresight, and provision is made for remote conditions, they are still such as will be the natural outgrowth of the present, and germinally contained in it. This is the case with the law of the kingdom (chap. 17) and of prophecy (18). The prophetic eye saw the future in the present, since the former was conditioned by the latter. This accounts for the emphasis laid on centralization of worship, and for the possibility of making regulations now which could be used centuries after as reformatory rules.

(5) The same principle may have caused the general treatment of certain classes — e.g., the priests as Levites — and a few other peculiarities. We are now enabled to put the question more definitely. Does the diversity of character preclude the unity of authorship? In other words, is it unthinkable that one and the same person should combine in himself the qualifications of a legislator and a prophet? That the modern criticism has answered this question in the negative, is enough to show how incapable it is of a deeper philosophical conception and appreciation of the Old Testament. It deals with phenomena as if they were the ultimate data; mathematical figures, which can be made to represent whatever value the critic ascribes to them. At the bottom of all this lies the naturalistic denial of those great principles whose recognition is absolutely necessary to a right understanding of the Old Testament. "In all induction, theory leads." Dr. Kuenen himself declares it impossible to argue from facts alone. He admits, that from certain indubitable points the chief lines must be drawn, and that these must guide in our interpretation of the rest. But whilst he accuses Schrader of having disregarded this principle, we might retort the charge upon himself and the newer criticism in general. In using the facts to establish its theory of development, this criticism has already violated the rule, that they are not to be interpreted outside of their legitimate sphere, or in the light of a naturalistic philosophy, but by the relation they sustain to the system of God's revelation of which Scripture is the record.

We believe, that, on the basis of a sound psychology, nothing can be said against the union of these qualifications in Moses. The example of Ezekiel, of whose Thora the critics have made such an extensive use, is enough to decide the question. Looked at from an historical standpoint, the combination was favored by all the circumstances. Israel was at the eve of a new period in its history, which would bring the final realization of long delayed promises, but at the same time expose to new and unknown allurements from the heathen world. It entered with the possession of Canaan upon a crisis of the same kind as those which in later ages called forth the warning and consoling voice of prophecy. It would have been anomalous, had it made this transition so far-reaching in its consequences without the attending light of a prophetical interpretation of the law to guide it. Not less obvious were these circumstances with regard to Moses himself, which favored this result. He had now nearly attained the end of his labors; and as, before his death, he saw the promised land from the top of Nebo, so in the sphere of time the range of his vision is widened. As the dying patriarchs saw and foretold the future fate of their descendants, and blessed their house in their last moments, so Moses, the greatest of all Old-Testament saints, left to the whole house of Israel, as a dying father, the best of all blessings, a law adapted to all future conditions. His work was not for one generation: "mediator of the Old Covenant," he stands high above all other prophets and saints; already half glorified, no longer subject to the limitations of time, he surveys the Israel of all ages until the coming of Christ, and accordingly his work assumes a prospective and ideal character, so striking that unbelieving critics could not but mistake it as the evidence of a much later origin.

Even a man like Dr. Kuenen admits that these formal characteristics of Deuteronomy do not necessarily prove that it was written by another hand than the intermediate books. It is only in connection with other material points that they obtain significance and convincing power. We need not examine all the arguments that have been adduced to prove the diversity of authorship, such as the peculiar style and language, the silence of Deuteronomy with regard to certain laws, the modification of previous laws, addition of some entirely new laws, etc. Some of these points have been partially discussed before; and all of them have been so exhaustively treated by Hengstenberg, Hävernick, Keil, Schultz, and others, that our remarks could be nothing more than a repetition of their statements.

We pass on to the second question involved: —

2. To which of the two legislations (that of the intermediate books, or of Deuteronomy) shall we assign the priority?

It might appear almost unnecessary after having thus defined the relation of Deuteronomy to the other Codes, to put the question just stated. If our conception of the book as prophetical is in the main correct, and verified by its applicability to the phenomena, this will decide the matter at once. Prophecy presupposes the law, — roots itself in it, and grows out of it. The legal and formal is before the spiritual and ideal, not in the mind of God, but in its historical realization. Nevertheless, since the history of modern criticism is very instructive on this special point, and a fair exponent of its unreliable character, we offer a few remarks.

1. In 1861 Dr. Kuenen gave the following comment on the views of Von Bohlen, George, and Vatke, who asserted that the Deuteronomic legislation was earlier than that of the middle books of the Pentateuch: "He [George] assumes that the historical elements of the Pentateuch are the oldest, that Deuteronomy was written during the reign of Josiah, whilst the greater part of the laws in Exodus-Numbers did not exist until after the exile. His arguments are partly external, partly internal; i.e., derived from a comparison of the two legislations. (1) Jeremiah, who knows Deuteronomy and makes frequent use of it, shows no acquaintance with the laws in Exodus-Numbers, as appears from chap. 7:21-23, where he appeals to Deut. 7:6, 14:2, 26:18, but

ignores the whole sacrificial Thora. But Jeremiah could, as Hosea, Isaiah, and other prophets before him, exalt the moral commands of the law far above its ceremonial prescriptions, and consider the former as the real basis of the Covenant with Jahveh, without the implication that a ceremonial Code did not yet exist in his time: he could even pronounce his conviction, that the laws concerning burnt-offering and sacrifice are later than the moral commands, and still it would not follow from this that Exodus-Numbers were committed to writing later than Deuteronomy. (2) Internal evidence. The priority of Deuteronomy is argued on the ground of several strange assertions, *which are not worthy of refutation;* to wit, that before the Babylonish captivity, there was no distinction between priests and Levites, high-priest and priests; that the Mosaic tabernacle never existed; that the spirit and tendency of Deuteronomy indicate an earlier period than those of Leviticus. Deut. 31:14 is considered wholly arbitrarily as a later addition: 18:2, 24:8, are left out of view. The view of George in this form as presented by him has been almost universally rejected."

So far Dr. Kuenen. The quotation is instructive in many respects. It proves (*a*) That a critic may proclaim as incontestable truth at one time what, a decade before, he deemed unworthy of refutation. (*b*) That he may use the same statements at different times to establish views which are diametrically opposed to each other (this with regard to Deut. 18:2, 24:8). (*c*) That he may propose, as a reasonable explanation of certain phenomena, what he condemns afterwards as uncritical dogmatism in others (this with regard to Jeremiah). (*d*) That so long as his mind is unbiased by preconceived philosophical theories, he may find the postulates of his own later philosophy absurd. (*e*) That consequently his theory is not determined by the facts, but that the facts are colored by a theory framed independently of them, and afterwards imposed upon them.

2. This is not the only instance, however, in which criticism has itself closed the way to its own later development, which it was not far-sighted enough to discern sufficiently long in advance. It is well known that Graf in 1866, five years after the appearance of Kuenen's introduction, declared the legislation of the middle books posterior to that of Deuteronomy. Connected with this was the statement that Deuteronomy presupposed not only the Jehovistic, but (*a potiori*) also the Elohistic, narrative. Pp. 9-19 of Graf's book contain an elaborate argument to prove that the narrative of the Elohist in Exodus-Numbers was known and used by the Deuteronomist. It was shown no less in detail that the Deuteronomist did not know the Levitical Code. It was evident, however, that in the Elohistic document, narrative and legislation were so indissolubly blended, that even the most daring critic could not sever them. This state of affairs was soon realized. Kuenen immediately discovered the weak point in Graf's hypothesis, and called his attention to it in a letter. Now, when two mutually inconsistent propositions have been independently established by an elaborate survey of facts, the natural suggestion

would be, to reject the whole process of criticism, that had led to such results, as unreliable. Instead of doing this, however, Kuenen advises Graf to extend his hypothesis to the narrative of the Elohist also. This advice was followed; and out came the present theory of Wellhausen, Kuenen, etc. We ask what has become in the mean while of Graf's arguments apparently so conclusive, that the Elohistic narrative was known to Deuteronomy? Have they been carefully reviewed? Not in the least. Dr. Kuenen simply declares it necessary, that either the laws should follow history, or history follow the laws. Here, however, criticism has denied its own principles. Whosoever claims to argue from facts, is not allowed to discard one of his conclusions to save another. If two conclusions are mutually exclusive, then nothing remains but to declare the whole argument invalid. We have exactly the same right to ignore Graf's proofs that the Deuteronomist shows no acquaintance with the Levitical law, in order to recognize merely his arguments that he knew the Elohistic narrative, and then, after the innocent remark that the laws must follow history, to consider the pre-Deuteronomic existence of the whole Priest Code established. But the idea of one thing "following" the other has no legitimate place in the sphere of criticism.

When placed in the light of the two facts just mentioned, the following considerations obtain a double force: — 1. The fact that Deuteronomy, on the whole, attaches itself to the Jehovistic Code, is no proof that the Levitical law did not then exist. The Covenant-law furnished the real basis for the Covenant between God and the people. It is no more than natural that Deuteronomy, wishing to bring out the fundamental ideas of this Covenant-relation in their spiritual bearing upon the popular life, should go back to the Code in which they were already germinally contained.

2. Whilst, in most cases, it is difficult to decide how two laws stand related to each other, it is quite different with history. One clearly stated proof that the Deuteronomist knew the narrative of the Elohist, is enough to settle the matter. But numerous proofs have been given by Graf and others. It is therefore safer to abandon the ambiguous method of ascertaining the relative age of two laws by a comparison of their contents, and to adhere to the results obtained from history, than the reverse.

3. (a) There are some indications, however, that Deuteronomy knows the Elohistic legislation. Attention has been called by the critics from a stylistic point of view to the frequent combinations חֻקּוֹת (*statutes*), מִצְוֹת (commandments), מִשְׁפָּטִים (*judgments*), תּוֹרָה (law), עֵדוּת (*testimony*). When we remember that the statutes of the Covenant-law are pre-eminently called מִשְׁפָּטִים (*judgments*), Exod. 21:1, and that the other terms are predominantly used of the Levitical legislation, then their combination in Deuteronomy becomes highly significant. Besides, it gives us the impression that the author of the latter had a voluminous body of law in mind, to which he referred the people. It is unnatural to refer the terms he uses to the scanty con-

tents of the Jehovistic Code (Exod. 13, 20-23, 34).

(*b*) The two laws (Lev. 11 and Deut. 14:3-21) are so similar in language and contents, that their interdependence cannot be doubted. Graf assigns the priority to Deuteronomy. This view is at once overthrown by the considera- tion that the language is Elohistic, and is accordingly in its place in the Priest Code, and out of place in Deuteronomy. Graf seeks to relieve this difficulty by assuming that both the Elohist and the Deuteronomist drew from an older source, but there is not the least ground for this assumption. And how this older source came to possess such a remarkable resemblance in language and contents to the Priest Code of much later date, remains a profound mys- tery. Moreover, the originality in the Priest Code is clear, because the refer- ence to the touching of a dead carcass does not coincide with the plan of Deu- teronomy, which is only to give law about clean and unclean food, but agrees perfectly with the plan of the Priest Code, which is to treat of every kind of defilement.

(*c*) Other cases of interdependence in which the priority of Leviticus is clear are Lev. 19:19 = Deut. 22:9-11, Lev. 19:13 = Deut. 24:14, Lev. 19:35 = Deut. 25:13-16.

(*d*) That Deuteronomy alludes to the priesthood of Aaron and Eleazar (10:6), to the Urim and Thummim (33:8), and to the priestly inheritance (10:9, 12:12, 14:27, 29, 18:1), has been pointed out before.

(*e*) The passages, Deut. 24:8, and 31:14, are even by Dr. Kuenen admitted as proof for the priority of Leviticus. When Kayser sees no reference in the former passage to the law of leprosy in Lev. 13, 14, but assumes that some other law may have been alluded to just as well, this other law exists only in his imagination, and there is not the slightest trace of its actual existence.

(*f*) A comparison of Deut. 28 with Lev. 26 will show that the Deuteronomist knew the latter discourse, or rather that both proceeded from the same au- thor; in which case the priority of the chapter in Leviticus as the shorter one is, of course, beyond dispute.

(*g*) Lev. 17 and Deut. 12 leave no doubt, both as to their mutual relation and their Mosaic origin.
Without the Levitical law being presupposed, that in Deuteronomy could have no meaning. Deuteronomy here abolishes in the fortieth year what the Priest Code had enacted in the second. The same relation exists between Deut. 4:41, 19:1-13, and Num. 35, treating of the cities of refuge.

(*h*) A reference to the ark in chap. 10:1 points back to Exod. 25:10.

4. All these cases, in which Deuteronomy makes short, incomplete, and ev- idently supplementary statements in regard to matters not treated by the Jehovist, are so many proofs of the priority of the Priest Code.

5. It was generally acknowledged that Deuteronomy throughout presup- poses the Levitical legislation, until theoretical bias obliged the critics to de- ny it. Even a man like De Wette once declared, "Deuteronomium prioribus libris tamquam fundamento niti quaevis pagina docet."

Chapter Fourteen - Internal Evidence for the Mosaic Origin of the Deuteronomic Code

We have come to the conclusion, that, whilst the unity of the Codes is vouched for by all evidence that can be reasonably demanded, the arguments adduced against it, when considered each on its own merits, cannot stand the test of a fair criticism. We could sum up the result in the statement, that the newest phase of Pentateuch-criticism presents no theory, but merely a hypothesis, one of the many ways of accounting for a number of facts. We believe that we have shown that the old hypothesis, if we may indeed call it so, accounts for these facts just as well as the new one, and in many respects better.

But it is not a matter of indifference which of the two hypotheses we shall choose. For whilst the new one must stand or fall on the mere merits of its plausibility and applicability, the old one has all the advantage of the direct testimony of the law itself, which lifts it out of the category of hypotheses, so that it becomes a theory founded on such facts as will admit no other interpretation.

For the whole Deuteronomic Code, we have in chap. 31:9, 24, the explicit testimony, that it was not only promulgated, but committed to writing, by Moses himself. With this statement, to be sure, nothing is decided as to the authorship of Deuteronomy as a whole. We may have our peculiar views, like Delitzsch and Kleinert, with regard to the composition of the book as a whole, and still agree on the fact, that Moses actually delivered these discourses. The only question that must be considered here, is whether the statements in ver. 9 and 24 do, or do not, refer to the whole Pentateuch. On this point, there is considerable difference of opinion. Hengstenberg, Hävernick, Keil, Schultz, etc., extend them to the whole Pentateuch, with the exception of the closing sections of Deuteronomy. Delitzsch, Kurtz, and, of course, the whole host of modern critics, limit them to the legal discourses of Deuteronomy. The latter view seems to be the most plausible one, for the following reasons: —

1. The passages 29:19, 26, 19:10, 30:20, 28:58, 61, suffer no other interpretation than that they refer to the Deuteronomic Code. From analogy we would expect the same to be intended here. Schultz admits this, but, since Deuteronomy proper does not extend beyond chap. 30, claims that the rest is written as a closing section of the whole Thora, and may accordingly refer to it as a whole. If such were the case, however, we would naturally first expect a direct statement that Moses committed Deuteronomy to writing, before it could be tacitly included under the general term of the Thora as a written whole. As this is nowhere found, and 30:1 speaks simply of Moses having *spoken* all these words, we must seek it in ver. 9 and 24.

2. It is not impossible, still it is improbable, that the delivering of this law mentioned in ver. 26 was a mere symbolic act, as the other view implies.

3. It was the special duty of the priests to preserve the law, and more especially the Levitical law was entrusted to them. We must therefore suppose that the latter had been delivered to them long before. If it be said that this may have been a mere copy of the Code, but that now the historical work of the Pentateuch was handed to them, we may answer that this analogy makes it only the more probable, that also the Deuteronomic Code was at first put into their hands separately without its historical frame.

4. The passage 29:1 shows that the Covenant made in the fields of Moab is considered as a separate one, distinct from that contracted at Horeb. There is no reason, then, to deny, that, according to the analogy of הַבְּרִית הַזֹּאת (this covenant), also הַתּוֹרָה הַזֹּאת (this law) means simply the Deuteronomic law.

5. Josh. 8:32 can hardly mean that the whole Pentateuch was written in stones on Mount Ebal. Keil claims that the expression used in Deut. 27:2, 8, "All the commandments, which I command you this day," is clearly intended to indicate, that here the whole Pentateuch is not meant, and that for this reason it does not decide any thing for the less explicit statements in other passages. But chap. 28:1 shows that the addition of "this day" cannot have been made for this special purpose. We have, therefore, a right to consider the passages where it is found as parallel to all the others, and find in them a confirmation of our view that also the latter speak only of the Deuteronomic Code.

It appears, then, that, from Deut. 31:9, 24, no direct argument for the Mosaic origin of the other Codes can be obtained. It does contain, however, an indirect testimony. If the Deuteronomic discourses were committed to writing immediately after their deliverance, we may infer *a potiori,* that Moses did the same with regard to the previous laws. That such was his custom, as it was the last thought at the end of his life, shows how much he laid to heart the careful preservation of the Codes.

Since the modern critics find themselves at liberty to disbelieve this explicit self-testimony of the Deuteronomic Code, there should be a strong weight of evidence to the contrary. Before we proceed to examine this, it is important to realize fully what such a disbelief involves; for on it will depend how much contrary evidence we demand in order to be convinced.

The term "literary fiction" has found large acceptance with the critics to designate their pretended origin of Deuteronomy. It does not fully suit the case, however. Again and again, critics have been anxious to remind us that the ideas of literary property were not so developed in antiquity as they are in our days. The Book of Deuteronomy, presenting itself to us as the work of Moses, has been compared to a parable; and Robertson Smith declares, that it matters little "whether these things were spoken by Moses literally, or in a parable." Dr. Kuenen, at least, is fair enough to confess that the fiction of the Deuteronomist cannot be defended from our stand-point of morality, but hastens to add, that a writer in the time of Manasseh cannot be measured by our moral standard. We must acknowledge, he says, that such a *pia fraus* was in those days quite consistent with a high degree of religious development.

Before proceeding farther, we must distinguish between a literary fiction and a legal forgery. When Riehm draws a parallel between Ecclesiastes and Deuteronomy, and then puts the question, "Why should we grant this liberty to the philosopher, and deny it to the lawgiver and prophet?" he has himself already intimated the answer that should be given to such questions. Suppose that Ecclesiastes were a literary fiction, still we could not blame the author for having introduced his work under the name of Solomon, because the fictitious character was not concealed, but intended to be understood and appreciated. On the other hand, there is every possible proof that the author of Deuteronomy wished his work to pass for the genuine work of Moses. The element of "falsehood" would be surely involved here. Most decisive in this respect is his statement that Moses *wrote* this law; also the fact that he does not allow any additions or subtractions or modifications to be made in what he gives as the words of Moses, 4:2, 12:32. How can we free from the charge of deceit, him who condemns most emphatically in his book a practice of which the book itself was the product? Further, the writer of Ecclesiastes would have given nothing more than subjective human speculation, under the authority of Solomon, since he need not have had the intention of foisting his book into the Canon. But the Deuteronomist applied his fictitious methods in the sphere of divine authoritative law, and knew, if he succeeded, that the first result of his success would be a deception of men in their most holy interests, an adulteration of the Canon, and in its ultimate analysis an encroachment upon God's sovereign right to prescribe law to Israel. It would be necessary to think that the times of Manasseh and Josiah were like the nineteenth century, when those initiated into the secrets of criticism do not hesitate to laugh contemptuously within the walls of their schools at the superstition of God's common people, who still cling to the antiquated notion of the Mosaic origin of the Pentateuch. The writer of Deuteronomy must have had some resemblance to our present heroes of Old-Testament science, who for themselves having long outgrown the traditional notions, still, out of the fullness of their benevolence, are willing to leave the less instructed class a kind of regulative knowledge. It is exceedingly saddening in the present state of the question, whilst the one alternative is "*fraud*," that even a man like Dr. Delitzsch declares that the Church at large has no interest in the Pentateuch question, and ought not to have. It is no longer the time to mislead ourselves by unmeaning phrases. The Church has an interest in this matter. If she has been deceived by the Deuteronomist more than twenty-five centuries ago, it is more than time that she knew it now. With Dr. Kuenen we say it is "either one thing or the other," and every attempt at compromise involves a concession to our opponents.

Before we hear the grounds on which critics think themselves justified in assuming this terrible fraud, let us survey the indirect testimony of Deuteronomy to its Mosaic origin.

1. The time in which the author speaks is evidently the later part of Moses' life. The people appear to be on the point of crossing the Jordan, the conquest of Canaan is promised as the reward of fidelity to Jehovah, the people are encouraged not to dread the Canaanites, commanded to extirpate the Canaanites, etc. To quote passages is superfluous.

2. The author shows intimate acquaintance with the geographical condition of the country in which Israel received this law. Whilst his statements concerning the eastern side of the Jordan betray by their minuteness and accuracy an eye-witness, those concerning the west side are general throughout.

3. When Riehm and others ascribe all this to the endeavor of the Deuteronomist to make his work pass for that of Moses, all the evidence is against them. For (*a*) The information concerning the Mosaic period is in part new, not contained in the previous books of the Pentateuch; and there is no proof that the Deuteronomist used other sources. (*b*) The history, though conforming to that of Exodus-Numbers, is remodeled with a freedom that nobody would have allowed himself to use in post-Mosaic times, least of all a writer who wished to authenticate his work with the impress of a genuine Mosaic character, and who everywhere proclaims the sacred, inviolable character of the Mosaic law. (*c*) It should be noticed, that all these references to the Mosaic period present themselves as natural and unintentional. If we had to assume that they were interwoven with a purpose, we would expect them to be more explicit, prominent, and emphatic.

4. Though Deuteronomy presupposes throughout the possession of the promised land, the point of view is never lost, that the conquest is still future. The possibility of fiction is precluded here by the promise of extended territory (11:24, "From Lebanon, from Euphrates, unto the uttermost sea"), such as even the most visionary expectations of later times could not have aspired to. How could a contemporary of King Manasseh or Josiah say, "From the river Euphrates shall your coast be," without exposing himself to ridicule?

5. Retrospectively the Code contains many references to the sojourn in Egypt of such a character as only the national consciousness in the Mosaic period could understand or appreciate. Memory of the Egyptian bondage is made an incentive to kind treatment of servants and strangers. The book is full of Egyptian reminiscences (11:10, 20:1, 23:4, 7, 24:22). The modern criticism has attributed all this to mercantile intercourse with Egypt. Apart from the fact, that in this case the allusions would have been more direct and intentional, the explanation is only a partial one. Mercantile intercourse was not adapted to make the reminder of Egyptian servitude a forcible incentive to humane treatment of servants. Neither would it account for historical coincidences, since there is no proof that intercourse with Egypt led to a professional study of Egyptian history and antiquities.

Chapter Fifteen - Objections Answered

All this, however, is most daringly rejected by the critics, as the product of a legal fiction which took to itself a Mosaic dress, thus to have better opportunity of imposing upon the people. Though there is some difference of opinion as to the exact date of composition, all agree that it is a Reform Code prepared in the days of the later Judaic kings. De Wette, Knobel, Schrader, Kayser, assign it to the reign of Josiah; Ewald, Bleek, Kuenen, to that of Manasseh; Riehm, who also first declared himself in favor of the second half of Manasseh's reign, afterwards changed his opinion, and preferred the time of Hezekiah. A peculiar view is held by Stähelin and Kleinert, that it was written during the period of the Judges.

When we ask for the proof of all this, it is arrayed before us in a series of propositions. Riehm's treatise affords a fair example of the common method. He proves in succession: 1. Deuteronomy is not Mosaic, but written a considerable time after the conquest of Canaan. 2. After the reign of Solomon. 3. Not before that of Jehoshaphat. 4. Not before that of Hezekiah. 5. In the second half of the reign of Manasseh, between 667 and 640. All which is inferred from internal evidence and corresponding facts in history during the period of the Kings.

That this method of determining the date of origin of a prophetical book involves a denial of its supernatural character, is obvious. When Deuteronomy prohibits exactly those things in which Solomon transgressed, it is claimed that there must be a *vaticinium ex eventu.* So far as these assertions proceed on the denial of the supernatural element in the history of Israel, no common ground of debate is left between us and the critics.

But there are others, like Riehm and Kayser, who recognize the supernatural element, and profess to derive their conclusions, not from an a priori philosophy, but from critical premises. Between them and us the question is reduced to the simple statement, whether these utterances of Deuteronomy exhibit the internal character of *vaticinia ex eventu,* or of real inspired prophecies.

Let us consider the law of the kingdom first. Chap. 17:14-20 offers several points of contact with Solomon's reign: 1. Multiplication of horses, ver. 16. 2. Multiplication of wives, ver. I7a. 3. Of silver and gold, ver. 17b. These points would certainly have some force to convince us, if it could be shown that Solomon's conduct in this respect was exceptional and distinct from what Eastern monarchs were accustomed to do. If not, there is no reason why Moses should not have dreaded for a king of Israel, what was prevailing at all Oriental courts, and hit upon exactly those vices which foreign influence afterwards tempted Solomon to imitate, in spite of the Deuteronomic law. That the author of 1 Kings 10:26-29, 11:2, uses nearly the same terms as Deuteronomy, does not prove that the latter merely copied the facts. The author of Kings may just as well have clothed the facts in Deuteronomic language.

When Riehm objects that he evidently describes with admiration and approval the *luxus* of Solomon's courts, and hence was not acquainted with the disapproval and condemnation of the law, this sounds strange in the mouth of a critic who declares in a footnote, that the writer of Kings did not live before the exile. Then, he must have known Deuteronomy, after all; and what becomes of the argument from approval or admiration?

The narrative of 1 Sam. 8 has also been used, or rather abused, to deny the authenticity of this law. What is there condemned, is here commanded. But such a summary statement leaves out of account several facts. First of all, Deuteronomy does *not command,* but merely allows, the institution of the kingly office. It does this with certain restrictions touching the points which would tend to make the office an object of national pride, derogatory to the honor of God, to whom alone such glory was due among Israel. The passage bears all the evidence of being a restrictive law. In one sense a kingdom is permitted, but evidently this permission is but subsidiary to the prohibition of it in another sense. It is clearly stated what the Israelites would be allowed to have, in order to bring out more emphatically and distinctly what they would *not* be allowed to desire. So, whilst there is no command in either sense, the whole is equivalent to a prohibition in the one sense. The restrictions stated constitute the very essence of kingly pride among the heathen nations of the East. Considered in this light, the Deuteronomic law not merely does not contradict, but strikingly confirms, the narrative in Samuel. The people desired exactly that kind of royalty which the Code prohibited, and from the very motive which the law condemned. Because the nation wished to transfer the national pride which it should have had in God alone to an earthly monarch, the spirit of the law was violated, even though the transgressors dared to quote its letter in their favor. That other causes cooperated with this to make the desire sinful, is not denied. Schultz has discussed the matter very thoroughly, though he seems to seek the solution rather in a peculiar interpretation of 1 Sam. 8 than of Deuteronomy.

The law presents no features which are not fully consistent with its Mosaic origin. But it contains some statements which are inconsistent with a later origin. The following may be noted: (*a*) The prohibition to confer royal authority upon a stranger, ver. 15. For this the whole post-Mosaic period offers no single point of contact. What Professor Robertson Smith adduces, rests on the misinterpretation of an isolated passage, Isa. 7:6. (*b*) The reminiscence of Egyptian servitude, ver. 16. How the multiplication of horses could tend to make the people return to Egypt, has never yet been satisfactorily explained on the critical hypothesis. Riehm's explanation, together with his view of the passage 28:68, rests on ingenious but unwarranted combinations, by which more is assumed than history has recorded. (*c*) If this law had been forged in a time when the kingly office had existed for many centuries, it is impossible that no more definite and concrete statements should have been made.

The same remarks apply to the institution of Judges, and of what the critics would call a supreme court (Deut. 17:8-13). Both are the necessary result of the people being scattered over the land immediately after the conquest. Here also the critics have substituted for this very natural interpretation an extremely forced one. They claim that Deuteronomy gives only the abstract statement of what Jehoshaphat had introduced in the concrete. But law and history conflict in so many points, that only a superficial acquaintance with both can make the one the reflex of the other. The following are essential differences: (*a*) Deuteronomy presents as future what under King Josiah had already existed for a considerable time. (*b*) What Jehoshaphat instituted was really a supreme court, consisting of Levites and laymen, with two presidents, — the high-priest Amariah, and Zebadiah the son of Ishmael. Deuteronomy knows nothing of this: the judge in ver. 9 is only the occasional president at the local court at the seat of the sanctuary, and he owes his right of decision in cases of appeal to his benefit of priestly assistance and instruction. The high-priest in ver. 12 is not introduced as such, but merely in his priestly capacity, to indicate that his assistance was not a matter of judicature, but of instruction. (*c*) The absence of concrete and detailed statements is here also a strong testimony against later origin.

As the law of the kingdom does not warrant us in bringing Deuteronomy down to Solomon's time, so that of the Judges does not prove its origin during or after the reign of Jehoshaphat. More general, but most whimsical and worthless of all, is the argument derived from the promises in chap. 18, that prophets like Moses would succeed him, and specially the reference to false prophets from ver. 20 onward. By remanding all this to a later time, we take away the only basis on which to rest prophecy. The eminent position and undisputed authority of later prophetism become a mystery when the law had made no provision for both. This is an apt illustration of the untenable positions to which the critical theories lead. If, as has been customary of late, prophecy is not considered as the fruit and interpreter of law, but law as the petrifaction of prophecy, the latter of necessity comes to hang in the air. The reference to false prophets, if it proves any thing, will prove against the later origin. In ver. 22 the people are exhorted not to be afraid of them, לֹא תָגוּר כִּמֶּנּוּ. In what a contrast does this supposed denunciatory character of the false prophets stand to the later reality! (compare 1 Kings 22:22, *seqq.* Isa. 9:15; 30:10; Jer. 14:13, 14). Another feature which forbids us to think that the author had the development of prophetism behind him, is the promise that the prophets would be like unto Moses. So only God and Moses could speak. None of the later prophets ever thought of claiming equality with Moses.

In Deut. 4:19, 17:3, star-worship is emphatically forbidden. The historical books mention, that after the schism it became prevalent at first in the Northern kingdom, afterwards also in Judah, in the time of Ahaz and Manasseh. Hence the critics inferred, that this kind of idolatry was not of Canaanitish origin, but was imported from the Far East, and not known before the schism. The protest of Deuteronomy against it then proves its later origin. We need not determine to what influences the increasing popularity of star-worship under the later kings was due, but have only to show that prior to this star-worship existed. This does not merely follow from the second command of the Decalogue forbidding to make a likeness of any thing "in heaven above," but also from the statement of Amos 5:26. The prophets of the Assyrian period refer to it; e.g., Isa. 17:8 (where the Revised Version has sun-images). Also the name Beth-shemesh (house of the sun) is noteworthy in this respect. Schultz calls attention to the fact that the service of Baal and Astarte was connected with star-worship; but, as Deuteronomy treats of this idolatry separately (4:3, 12:31, 18:20), the passage (4:19) must refer to something distinct from it. That Deuteronomy considers this cult under the aspect of nature-worship, and not so much of Polytheism as it came pre-eminently to be afterwards, makes the acquaintance of the writer with this later state of affairs improbable.

The phrase הַיַּרְדֵּן בְּעֵבֶר (beyond Jordan) has been appealed to as indicating the true stand-point of the later writer. It is used interchangeably of the east and the west side of the river. In making this fact a proof of later origin, the critics involve themselves in a serious difficulty. All evidence of Mosaic origin is summarily dismissed with the remark, that the Deuteronomist would take care to reproduce faithfully the Mosaic situation. In all other instances he succeeded so completely, that for centuries all critical opinion was led astray by his fiction. How, then, could he fall out of his *role* here? Even granted that Deuteronomy is non-Mosaic, the double sense in which the writer employs the phrase puts beyond doubt that he considered it as geographically fixed already in the Mosaic time. Still, it is most probable that even in this case he would not have made Moses employ it of the east side, for fear that people less instructed in ancient geographical terminology might suspect the Code on account of this expression. Riehm, feeling this, tries to protect the Deuteronomist against this charge of thoughtlessness, by saying that he continually distinguishes between his own work and the discourses of Moses, and that in the latter the phrase is only applied to the western country. Chap. 3:8 is enough to overthrow this notion, where Moses himself speaks "And we took...the land that was בְּעֵבֶר הַיַּרְדֵּן from the river of Arnon unto Mount Hermon." Riehm is under the necessity of declaring the latter words to be a gloss of a later hand; but with the same right we might declare all passages where the term is applied to the eastern country interpolations, which would certainly be the easiest way to relieve the whole difficulty. As the matter stands, the critics may choose between admitting that the Deuteronomist fell out of his *role* here, which will add the more weight to other evidence of Mosaic origin, or that he thought Moses could have spoken thus. We take the latter alternative in view of the impossibility that a man who wore his mask so well should have made such a blunder here, and be-

98

cause we do not see why Moses and the Israelites in general could not be familiar with a settled phrase like this. The western side was at all times, even from the days of the patriarchs, the real Canaan, the fixed point, determining the usage of all relative terms. Much more could it be so for Moses, who continually in the prophetic spirit transfers himself to the future time, and speaks for the period when Western Canaan would be already conquered and occupied.

We close with noticing a few positive arguments which make the later origin of Deuteronomy very improbable.

1. The military law of chap. 20, which commands emphatically the extirpation of the Canaanites, is out of place in the time after Solomon, since he made the remnant of Canaan's heathen inhabitants servants to Israel in a peaceful way. The warning against an idolatrous cultus may not have been superfluous at a later date; but the military law had become utterly unmeaning, and the latter could never have been used as a safeguard against the former. Professor Robertson Smith admits that "this feature points us directly back to the days of Moses."

2. The curse upon Amalek (chap. 25:17) leads to the same conclusion. According to 1 Chron. 4:43, the last remnant of the Amalekites was destroyed by the tribe of Simeon positively not later than the reign of Hezekiah, as even Graf and Kayser admit. That the passage is simply repeated from Exod. 17:14 will not help us. Kayser should have made clear what occasion there was in Josiah's time to make the repetition.

3. The hostile attitude towards the Ammonites prescribed in 23:3-6 could be explained just as well from the later times. Parallel passages are found in Jeremiah and Zephaniah. But the friendly feelings towards Edom lack all points of contact with the history of the seventh century. The same applies to the mention of Egypt (23:7). Until the destruction of Jerusalem the prophets speak of Edom as the representative of the enemies of God's people. A command, "thou shalt not abhor an Edomite," would be unparalleled in the prophetic literature of Israel. When Kayser tries to show that Judah was occasionally on friendly terms with Edom, his quotations do not prove this. Riehm infers from the tendency in Hezekiah's time to seek the alliance of Egypt, that this required a friendly relation to the Edomites, and that accordingly the Deuteronomist would recommend it. But both Kayser and Riehm have overlooked that Deuteronomy is written in a prophetic spirit, and could by no means approve of this tendency to lean upon Egypt, or favor any thing resulting from it, since all the prophets unanimously condemn such associations. It is therefore impossible that the writer should speak in such terms of Egypt. Josiah himself, whose conduct better expresses the theocratic spirit out of which Deuteronomy must have been written, according to the critics, opposed Egypt, and lost his life in doing so.

4. Deut. 12:15 contains a modification of the law Lev. 17), which was practicable only during the desert-journey, when the people lived in the immedi-

ate vicinity of the tabernacle. Its impracticability at any other time is self-evident. Even the plurality of sanctuaries afterwards would not have made it practicable, since they were by no means so numerous that all slaughtering of animals could be done in their neighborhood.

5. Several laws present features that become unintelligible in the light of later conditions. For instance, 20:5-8 makes military service almost a matter of free choice. How could this be in the warlike period of the later kings? Compare also 22:13-21, evidently an old custom, which must have been antiquated long before the seventh century; also 27:21.

6. Though Deuteronomy is eminently prophetical in one sense, it is in so far distinguished from the later prophets, as that no reaction appears against ceremonial formalism. This is an unequivocal sign that such a contrast did not yet exist. Positively the ideal character of the law is exhibited, but nowhere is observance of its external prescriptions negatively condemned. The critics, who make such an extensive use of this latter feature in their interpretation of the prophets, should at least have wondered why it is entirely lacking in Deuteronomy.

7. Finally, this fact speaks against a later origin, that, so far as would appear from Deuteronomy, the passing of Jordan, the complete conquest of Canaan, and its quiet, undisturbed possession, coincide. This is wholly inconsistent with the theory of historical retrospection. The latter knew that a long period had been necessary to subdue the Canaanites, and that the task was not fully accomplished before Solomon.

Chapter Sixteen - Internal Evidence of the Mosaic Origin of the Laws in Exodus-Numbers

If our belief in the Mosaic origin of the Deuteronomic Code rests on valid grounds, we have an *a potiori* argument for the authenticity of the laws contained in the middle books. Our work is rendered more easy and simple, because a great number of traces of later origin discovered by the critics in Deuteronomy are not found here.

1. We first state the direct testimony of the laws to their own origin, which is of a twofold character: (*a*) when simply Mosaic origin is claimed; (*b*) when it is explicitly stated that Moses committed certain laws to writing.

(*a*) A great number of laws are introduced by formulas like the following: "The LORD spake unto Moses." "And the LORD called unto Moses, and spake unto him out of the tabernacle of the congregation." "And he [Moses] said unto Aaron." "And the LORD spake unto Moses and to Aaron." "And the LORD spake unto Moses in Mount Sinai." These introductory statements cover the whole book of Leviticus, and in Numbers we find the same repeated throughout. All these laws claim for themselves Mosaic origin.

(*b*) The passages in which Moses is said to have committed certain laws to writing are the following:—

Exod. 17:14: "And the LORD said unto Moses, Write this for a memorial in a book, and rehearse it in the ears of Joshua: for I will utterly put out the remembrance of Amalek from under heaven." The statement falls outside of the Code, and is important for our present purpose only in so far as the book referred to might furnish an indirect testimony to the fact that Moses wrote the history of his lifetime. The Massorah has it, בַּסֵּפֶר (*in the book*), with the article. Though the presence or the absence of the article depends on the punctuation, still we may inquire whether the Massorah had no good grounds in putting it here, in spite of its omission in the Greek and Arabic translations (the only ones which could express it). For, as the punctuation without the article would have doubtless been the more natural one, its addition must have rested on positive reasons in the nature of the case. Now, we cannot but find it absurd to call a separate note of this character "a book," or even to preserve it as an isolated sentence in written form. The passages which Bleek adduces, do not prove that a single sentence committed to writing could constitute a book. One of them (Jer. 32:19) does not speak of a book, and the others refer to more comprehensive laws or decrees. The most plausible interpretation is that which the Massorah intimated by adding the article viz., that Moses was accustomed to commemorate important events and commands, and that this book, the origin of our present Pentateuch, is referred to by God.

Exod. 24:4: "And Moses wrote all the words of the LORD." The words of the Book of the Covenant are meant, which included chap. 20:22-23:33. Whether the Decalogue was included is not certain, but improbable for the following reasons: (*a*) The book was read in the audience of the people (ver. 7); this would have been superfluous in case of the Decalogue, which God himself had promulgated with audible voice. (*b*) It is not stated that Moses wrote the Decalogue: God himself wrote it on tables of stone. (*c*) The parallel Covenant-law in chap. 34, equally committed to writing, did not repeat the Decalogue.

Num. 33:2: Moses wrote the list of stations during the desert-journey (ver. 3-49).

These passages cover a comparatively small part of the Sinaitic legislation. Critics have rashly inferred that we have no positive testimony of its codification by Moses, and have even gone to the length of asserting that the passages just enumerated exclude the writing of any other part of the law by Moses. Dr. Kuenen says, "When in the first four books of the Pentateuch, only a few pieces of little length are ascribed to Moses, it becomes probable that all the rest, in the writer's opinion, is non-Mosaic." Delitzsch and Bleek and many others are of the same opinion.

We believe that this conclusion is as unwarranted as the other extreme, to which some conservative critics have gone, of asserting that we might reason, from the part being written by Moses, that the whole was. The truth is, that these passages prove nothing in either direction; since the special command to write was clearly occasioned by extraordinary circumstances, and served a special purpose. That Exod. 17:14 presupposes a more comprehensive work, we have seen already. The Covenant-law had to be written separately for its symbolic use in the solemn transaction (chap. 24). After the Covenant had been broken, the second law (chap. 34) was, of course, written separately after the analogy of the first.

There can be, then, no doubt that the Jehovistic and Elohistic legislation claim for themselves Mosaic origin. We must accept this self-testimony, so long as it has not been disproved by other evidence. Accordingly we might stop here, and, remembering how the unity of the laws in Exodus-Numbers has been established, dismiss the subject. Still, it may be well to survey the contents of the intermediate books with special regard to —

2. Their indirect internal evidence of Mosaic origin.

Many of the Levitical laws are so formulated, that they presuppose the sojourn of the people in the desert-camp around the tabernacle; and many commands rest for their practicability entirely on this situation. It is superfluous to point this out in detail. Compare Lev. 1-7, 11-16, 13, 14, 16, 17; Num. 1, 2, 4, 10:1-8, 19.

In the case of other laws, the form is determined by the historical event that occasioned them, so that they cannot have existed separate apart from the latter. Exod. 35-40 is thus connected with chap. 25-31. Lev. 16 attaches itself to chap. 10:1.

Bleek based on these facts the following propositions: —

1. Even if the Pentateuch in its present form be not composed by Moses, and it be shown that many individual laws are the product of a later time, still the Pentateuchal Code as a whole is, as to its spirit and character, genuine and Mosaic.

2. The art of writing must have been already known among the Hebrew people in the Mosaic period, and practiced to such an extent that comprehensive law-books were in existence.

3. We stand in the Pentateuch (as far as the middle books are concerned) throughout on an historical basis.

At first blush, it would seem that these positions were unassailable. The old way of speaking of myths, legends, or at best of traditions, so extensively applied to history, proved impracticable here. All the characteristics of myths and legends were wanting; and, as Wellhausen strikingly remarks, "For the originality of legends, exactly the opposite criteria decide from those by which actual history is tested. Legends are at the farthest distance from their source, where they appear in connection with an exact chronology." And so the case actually stands. The phenomena admit of only two theories for their explanation; more and more the extremes draw to themselves the occupants of abandoned intermediate positions; we have to choose between Baal and God, nature-worship and supernatural religion, fraud and history.

The modern criticism has not shrunk from taking the former of these alternatives. The Priest Code cannot be Mosaic. Still, it bears the impress of

Mosaic origin. To reconcile these two facts, only one way is left open: what is not genuine, and still so striking, must have been fabricated with a purpose; the Mosaic dress of the priestly laws is woven for it by the skillful hands of exilic and post-exilic fraud.

These extreme views seem to have no common ground left on which to meet each other. What we recognize as one of the most striking proofs of Mosaic origin, is immediately construed on the other side as the meanest sort of Judaizing fiction. The material, under the molding hands of criticism, is like clay in the hands of a potter. There is no manner of argumentation which is not instantly, under the influence of these profane principles, turned round in the opposite direction.

To decide this question critically, no amount of philosophy or religious conviction will suffice. It is only when on both sides the following principles are admitted, that there is some hope of an historical solution of the problem: —

1. A legal as well as a literary fiction, however ingeniously devised, will always more or less betray the time of its origin. The veil thrown over it will be so transparent in some spots, that the actual situation can be recognized. With regard to Deuteronomy, the whole critical argument rests on the validity of this principle. We do, therefore, no injustice to the critics in applying it here.

2. The fiction will naturally seize upon such points in the fictitious situation which it portrays, as stand in immediate contact with the present for which it tries to provide. The ideal is not for its own sake, but serves a practical purpose: it must accordingly be chosen so as to have a direct bearing upon the latter.

Even a superficial observer cannot but discover that the pretended Priest Code does not comply with either of these conditions. Numerous historical allusions, referring even to minute and unimportant points, as we saw, are discovered in Deuteronomy. Historical data are disentangled from their Mosaic environment, and successively assigned to their alleged true place in the history of later times. Riehm proves by a purely internal process, that Deuteronomy must have been written after the time of Solomon, Jehoshaphat, Hezekiah, Manasseh, in the reign of Josiah. Will the critics lay before us a similar series of propositions, that we may gradually and reasonably convince ourselves of the post-exilic origin of the Priest Code? No semblance of internal evidence is given, neither do the critics claim that any exists. There must certainly be a reason, if the Code originated between Ezekiel's Thora (B.C. 574) and its promulgation by Ezra (B.C. 444), a time of such critical and momentous changes in the history of Israel, — there must, we say, be a reason why it lacks all historical references. Had the art of forgery made such marvelous progress in the mean while, that, whilst the Deuteronomist still partially failed, the writers of the Priest Code fully succeeded in hiding themselves behind the shield of Moses?

What point of contact do the exilic and post-exilic times offer for Lev. 17? What practical bearing could such a law as that of chap. 16, concerning the Day of Atonement, have upon a period when the ark no longer existed? How can we find a positive reason for the forging of such commands? The cultus of the past was in many cases deficient, and could not furnish a norm. Neither did Ezekiel's Thora bind them. What other principle can have governed the framers of these laws, if not their adaptability to the future restoration? How, then, shall we account for the scene of the whole not being laid in Canaan, but in the desert, and, moreover, the laws being adapted to a large extent only to the desert-life? It is no answer to say that the fictitious character made such dissimulation necessary. The question is, why was exactly this form of dissimulation chosen? That the Mosaic mask could have been imposed on more attractive and appropriate features, the critical opinion of Deuteronomy shows. Why is not Moses represented as giving a law with special reference to the settled life of the people in Canaan? All these questions the newer criticism fails to answer. As it has stripped the Mosaic period of its miraculous character, so it has enshrouded the time of the exile and the subsequent period in an impenetrable mist.

We ask whether there are no portions of these laws whose authenticity can be established independently of this self-testimony, so that we may make them the basis for further argumentation. If only one case can be indicated where the internal evidence is verified beyond doubt by external considerations, the critical theory of fiction fails.

Now, there are such cases. The Mosaic institutions, as they are represented in the Codes, are full of Egyptian reminiscences. It is true, every resemblance does not justify us in assuming a historical connection, since certain rites and ceremonies are common to all ancient peoples. But in some cases the similarity may be so striking, and so strongly corroborated by historical testimony, that accident is out of the question. An illustration of this we find in the law concerning leprosy, and its treatment by the priests (Lev. 13, 14). The following facts, as stated by Delitzsch, concur to establish their Mosaic origin almost beyond dispute (*a*) The exodus of Israel has been identified by nearly all Egyptologists with the expulsion of the lepers spoken of by Manetho, Chaeremon, Lysimachus, Tacitus, Diodorus, and Justinus. (*b*) The peculiar form in which Egyptian tradition has preserved this memory of the exodus can only be accounted for by the assumption that leprosy prevailed more or less among the Israelites. Over-population, the result of their rapid increase in Goshen, may have been the natural cause of this impurity. This is confirmed by Scripture testimony of Jehovistic character (Exod. 4:6; Num. 12:10, 15). (*c*) On account of this plague, the Egyptians would necessarily consider the Jews as the importers of leprosy, and, as they carried their systematic purifications to an extreme for themselves, would exert an influence in the same direction upon the Israelites. (*d*) This sanitary, and more specially prophylactic, treatment of the disease was among the Egyptians assigned to the priests, and must have been pursued in accordance with certain fixed rules, as was the case with their medical practice in general. (*e*) It admits of no doubt, that the Israelites would follow in their treatment of the plague Egyptian usage. (*f*) Actually we find in their laws a carefully prescribed method of dealing with it; diagnostic criteria are given; it appears also as the special task of the priests, to discern the various phases of the disease, and declare the persons clean or unclean after a careful inspection. All these traits combined, amount almost to a logical demonstration of the Egyptian, and consequently Mosaic, origin of the law of leprosy.

That there was such a law prior to the Deuteronomic Code, the passage 24:8 shows. When the critics resort to the arbitrary assumption, that some other law may just as well have been referred to by the Deuteronomist, we have reached the sphere of the unknowable, where it is not safe to carry on the discussion.

This case of a clearly established Mosaic law within the limits of the Priest Code has significance in more than one respect. 1. As in the regulations, mention is made of the tabernacle of the congregation and of the camp (13:46, 14:11), we infer that such local specifications, when occurring elsewhere, are justly considered as internal marks of Mosaic origin, and that, in the main, the local coloring of these laws is not fictitious, but reliable. 2. The fact that the tabernacle appears here as a place of sacrifice in ver. 11, and not merely as a tent for consulting God, which, according to the critics, is its Jehovistic conception, proves that in the laws of the tabernacle and of the Aaronic priesthood we stand on historic ground. 3. The mention of the sin- and trespass-offering in chap. 14 is a proof that these two species of sacrifice were pre-exilic, and indeed Mosaic, in their origin, and not, as the critics assert, post-Ezekielian.

If any thing in this collection of laws is Mosaic, it will be the Decalogue. Belonging to what the critics themselves consider the oldest Code, and, according to the oldest history, being written on tables of stone by the finger of God, its simple form, early appearance, and indubitable presence in the ark in later time, all combine to render the highest antiquity plausible. To this may be added the remarkable fact, that the Decalogue of Exodus, though slightly differing in form from the Deuteronomic one, is nevertheless essentially Deuteronomic in language and expression. At the same time, it shows the usual characteristics of the Jehovist. What the critics adduce against its Mosaic origin, cannot outweigh these strong presumptions in favor of it. The alterations in the Deuteronomic text can only awake surprise when we assign as late a date to the composition of the book as the critics do. Moses' reproduction might be a free one, as his whole Deuterosis of the law evidently is. That the Deuteronomic Decalogue puts the Sabbath-law on another basis is inaccurate. The truth is, that the real foundation of the command is not restated, but a practical incentive substituted, — the reminder that the people had been servants in Egypt; and this reference to Egypt pervades the whole Code.

Another objection of Reuss, Wellhausen, etc., is, that the prohibition to worship God under an image cannot reach up to the time of Moses, and that the cultus instituted by Jeroboam after the schism proves its non-existence at that date. But the assertion that Jeroboam's cultus was not essentially new or exotic, but was customary long before in Canaan (R. Smith), cannot be proved. Neither did the earlier prophets tolerate the calf-worship, except as a lesser evil in contrast with the service of Baal and Astarte. The calf made in the wilderness by Aaron reminds us of Egypt: likewise Jeroboam's cultus probably proceeded from Egypt, where he had enjoyed the hospitality of the king. This transgression of a well-known command is not without parallel in history: certainly the Romish Church, in adoring Mary, the angels, and saints, shows no ignorance of the Decalogue. Just as well may Jeroboam have quieted his not too tender conscience by some forced interpretation of the law. The newer critics, who are inclined to leave to Moses as little as possible, generally make an exception in this case. Smend admits the Mosaic origin of the Decalogue unconditionally. Others with some restrictions. Graf conceded Mosaic origin in some original form, different from the one we possess now, and holds that the ten words were at first transmitted orally. Nöldeke is unwilling to grant even as little or as much as that; and Reuss, with Wellhausen, goes to the length of denying that Moses had any thing whatever to do with the Decalogue.

Chapter Seventeen - Testimony of the Historical Books – Judges, First and Second Samuel, First and Second Kings

The radical difference between our conception of the Old Testament and that of the critics is such that it makes historical argumentation extremely difficult, Of course, all depends on our estimate of the sources and here the disagreement begins already. Joshua is so dependent on the Pentateuch, that its testimony is *a priori* declared invalid. Judges has undergone various redactions, in which the historical truth was molded for religious instruction (Reuss, Gesch., p. 337). First, it consisted of a number of independent legends, lacking all unity except that of a common national spirit. They were collected into a body, and the religious tendency of the redactor furnished the thread of their connection. History was made revelation, says Reuss. "Judges is a prophetical sermon," To the author's generation, the old, heroic times had become quite unintelligible so that it devolves upon an omniscient criticism to correct in a pedantic schoolmasterly way the wrong conceptions entertained by the Israelites concerning their own history. The case stands no better with the books of Samuel and Kings (compare Reuss, §§ 245, *seqq.*, 340, *seqq.*). And how the newer criticism has dealt with Chronicles, is too well known to need special mention here.

From all this, it appears that to assail the critics on historical grounds is lost labor. They have their conception of the Old Testament, and we have ours. When, in Judges, certain deviations from the Mosaic law appear, often with the express disapproval of the author, all statements of the latter character are attributed to the redactor, who sees the facts in his own subjective light, so that the disapproval is not God's, but his. According to our view, the historical books were written with the very purpose of making past history a mirror and warning for the future Israel. According to the critics, all tendency towards instruction is of later date. In other words, we claim that the self-conscious, revealing God was in history from the beginning, and caused history to be written as such: the critics refuse to recognize any history as genuine except as it presents itself under the fascinating disguise of a legend or myth. All deeper conception of history is excluded. This amounts, of course, to a denial of the supernatural element in its course. But the fact remains, that it is a hopeless task to convince our opponents by adducing phenomena, because they will construe them according to their own theory, as we do according to ours. The illusion that theories are founded on facts, has to be given up: neither should it be so, for without more or less of preconceived hypothesis, the facts alone remain dark and indifferent.

For this reason, we think it useless to prove positively from the historical books, that, in the time of which they treat, the Pentateuchal Codes, or, even as Hengstenberg and others have attempted to demonstrate, the Pentateuch itself, existed. The direct testimonies collected from such passages as 2 Sam. 22:23; 1 Kings 2:3, 6:12, 8:53, are not of such a character, or so numerous, but the critics can help themselves with the assumption of a few interpolations. References to civil or ceremonial usages of similar character to those described in the Codes do not prove that the latter existed; for all the critics admit, e.g., that the ritual was pre-exilic in substance, though not codified before the exile. Only manifest verbal quotations would help; but these, again, are not numerous enough to warrant general and decisive conclusions and very seldom is the relation of two passages such that it permits only one view concerning their interdependence. We do not mean to say that the traces of the existence of a ritual, as they appear in the historical books, have no right to speak in this matter, but simply that they are no decisive proofs of the existence of the Pentateuchal Codes. Their value consists in the evidence they afford, that the ritualistic spirit was by no means exclusively the fruit and exponent of post-exilic Judaism, but one of the features of Jewish national life from the beginning. Israel was the people of the law long before the pretended origin of the Priest Code. And, in so far as the historical books bear testimony to this fact, they furnish abundant material for the construction of a solid argument against the newest phase of criticism. It should also be remembered, that the difference between ritualistic usage and ritual law is not so great as it is often represented by the critics. Every one who admits that a ritual existed corresponding to the *technique* of the Priest Code, has thereby taken our side with regard to the main question; and we will not dispute with him on the subordinate point, whether this usage was written or unwritten law. Usage, when once fixed, necessarily becomes law.

In the main, our attitude on this point must be apologetic. In making this concession, we can justly claim that the critics shall not construe the silence of history concerning any law as a proof of its nonexistence. We do not infer from the mention of some usage, that it was regulated by law. Neither should our opponents infer from the absence of such mention, that no law could have existed. For the rest, we simply try to show that the facts, which are admitted as historical on both sides, do *not exclude* the existence of the Pentateuchal Codes.

We begin with the period of Judges. That the people sacrificed at Bochim (2:5), Gideon at Ophrah (6:21), Manoah at Zorah (13:19), can by no means have involved a transgression of the law; for in all these instances, there was an appearance of the כְּלְאַךְ (*angel of Jehovah*); and the provisionary regulation given at Sinai, before the promulgation of the Levitical law, went into effect once more. That this is the true explanation, is specially seen from one fact generally overlooked; viz., that *no theophany took place without a sacrifice*, which shows how closely the ideas of a revelation made by God, and of a sacrifice made by man, were connected in the Israelitish mind so that we are not only warranted in thus harmonizing law and history, but positively claim that the right to sacrifice at an arbitrary place, as the critics postulate it, was utterly inconsistent with the most primitive elements of the Hebrew religious consciousness.

For Gideon's sacrifice (6:26), the peculiar circumstances and the symbolical significance are enough to make it an exceptional case. In the place where the idol had been served, Jehovah reclaimed what was his own. This nocturnal, private *olah,* on a spot whose vicinity had been shortly before sanctified by a theophany (ver. 11, *seqq.*), decides, of course, nothing as to the common practice.

In other passages, no mention of sacrifices is made. Gideon's altar was strictly memorial, as appears from the fact that (*a*) he gives it a name: altars erected for practical use had no names. (*b*) Until this day it is yet in Ophrah; i.e., as a memorial or ancient relic. (*c*) Gideon is commanded in ver. 26 to build a second altar, this time for a practical purpose. That in chap. 11:11, Jephthah is said to have uttered all his words before the LORD at Mizpeh, can be used on the critical side only by a double allegation: (*a*) that the swearing of an oath was necessarily connected with sacrifices, of which the preceding verse is already a flat contradiction; (*b*) that לִפְנֵי must refer to a sanctuary. It simply means, "as in the presence of Jehovah," a circumlocution for "taking Jehovah as witness," "testifying with invocation of his name"; i.e., "solemn swearing." Chap. 20:1 must and can be explained on the same principle. Neither does the narrative of chaps. 20, 21, afford any serious difficulty; for in 20:27 it is explicitly stated that the ark was in the vicinity with

Phinehas the priest, howsoever we may understand בֵּית אֵל (Bethel, or house of God) in ver. 26 and in chap. 21:2.

In other cases, where there is an actual transgression of the law, as that of Micah and the Danites, the censure of the writer is not only expressed in the whole tenor of the narrative, but also explicitly stated.

The objection that others than priests officiated in sacrificial transactions, has still less force. Gideon and Manoah offered, because Jehovah, in approaching them visibly, sanctioned an immediate exercise of that priestly right, which, belonging to all Israel, was only representatively vested in the Levitical priests. Wherever the LORD appears, there is his altar. To whomsoever he draws near, he gives the right to come near, which is the essence of the priesthood.

It is alleged that we do not get the impression from the first chapters of Samuel, that the elaborate Levitical law was in operation. This is certainly true but very little dependence can be placed on such an impression, which it certainly could not be the intention of the writer to convey. Who will be rash enough to infer, because Eli's sons are the only priests mentioned, that there were no others? From 1 Sam. 21 we get the impression that there was only a single priest, Ahimelech, at Nob. But chap. 22 takes away the impression by stating that not less than fourscore and five priests were slain by Doeg.

It was an old objection, already made by Gramberg, and now revived by Wellhausen and the newer school, that, in the oldest sacrificial *praxis,* the meat was boiled. 1 Sam. 2:15-I 7 is quoted as an example. But the most superficial inspection of the passage shows that there is no allusion to the offering of cooked flesh at all. Ver. 15 says, "Before they burnt the fat:" we have to do here with *shelamim*. The sin of the priests consisted in desiring their part before Jehovah. For the rest, the whole passage implies that the customs then in vogue at the sanctuary cannot be taken as exponents of the existing laws.

The circumstances of Samuel's time — first the captivity of the ark, afterwards its separation from the sanctuary, the general apostasy of the people — account for all the facts that confront us here. It has been asked, If unity of worship was the divine command, why was not the ark, after its return, restored to the sanctuary, and the centralization of sacrifices enforced? The answer is obvious. Then, as at all times, mighty reforms require a period of long inward preparation. To effect the latter was Samuel's mission, and to keep this in mind affords the only key to a right understanding of his whole life. This meets the critical objection, that, if Israel were deprived of a national sanctuary, all worship, at least sacrificial worship, ought to have ceased. Between Eli and David's time, this slow process of inward preparation went on; the spirit of reform was striving with the spirit of apostasy; all intermediate phenomena testify to an abnormal state. So at least the Old Testament itself considers it (Jer. 7:12, 14, 26:6; Ps. 78:60, 68). The transition was from Shiloh to Zion. What happened at both was legal, and does bear witness to the law: what falls between them was in part abnormal, in part illicit, and should not be made to testify against the law. Still, even here matters do not stand out in so bad light as critics represent them. When Saul undertakes to sacrifice, without waiting for Samuel's presence, he is severely rebuked; and this act becomes the turning-point in his life. This certainly does not look like a state of affairs in which everybody could sacrifice. When the author of the books of Samuel mentions with manifest approval, that Saul built an altar, this must be understood in the entire light of Saul's character: it expressed a sort of piety, though in a deficient form. What David did on the threshing-floor of Araunah was justified by the appearance of the angel, and the authority of a prophet of God, and was in anticipation of the erection of the sanctuary on that very spot. The repeated sacrifices on the high-place of Gibeon are accounted for by the presence of the tabernacle and *olah* altar (1 Chron. 16:39, 40). That David was accustomed to worship God on the top of the mount in the neighborhood of Jerusalem, does not imply that he sacrificed there. His ephod was not the high-priestly garment, but simply an ephod *bad;* that is, a linen ephod. The modification made by David in the age fixed for the Levites' entering upon the service at the sanctuary, is best explained by the change in the abode of the ark, which had now become a permanent one, so that the work of the Levites became easier, and the time of their service could be proportionally prolonged. Those who defend the post-exilic origin of the Priest Code may try their skill in harmonizing the passages 2 Chron. 31:17, and Ezra 3:8, which prove that not only in Hezekiah's time, but also in that of Zerubbabel, the limit was twenty years. Notwithstanding the prominent part taken by Solomon in the consecration of the temple, nothing is ascribed to him which would have been an intrusion upon the rights of the priesthood. For the true character of this whole period from a religious point of view, compare 1 Kings 3:2.

For the period succeeding the schism, the existence of a divinely authenticated law becomes a postulate without which the history is wholly unintelligible. This only could prevent the Northern kingdom from becoming fully apostate, and relapsing into complete heathenism. There was a restraining power, even in the worst days of the dynasty of Omri: there was what Elijah called a "halting between two opinions." It is, indeed, possible to find in all this nothing but the influence of long existing usage, owing its origin to the centralization in the days of David and Solomon. But, on the one hand, the period in which this *usus* should have gained ascendancy is far too short to account for the unwavering attachment which the pious in Israel retained to the sanctuary at Jerusalem: on the other hand, the reaction in the Northern kingdom opposed the modified cultus so long and so firmly, that it must have had a deeper source than the custom of a few decades; the only satisfactory explanation is, that it rooted in the divine Thora, and preserved a clear consciousness of this origin to the very last.

The objection was raised already by Eichhorn and Vatke, and afterwards has often been repeated, that the prophets of the Northern kingdom (Elijah and Elisha) did not oppose the idolatry of the golden calves, but simply Baal-worship. But obviously their opposition was determined by the sins that were most objectionable at the time; and, when Baal-worship had found such general acceptance, the idolatry of the golden calves became a comparatively unimportant affair. How the prophets who were not influenced by this excess of wickedness, judged of the plurality of altars and the worship of the calves, is seen in Amos, Hosea, and the Micaiah of 1 Kings 22. The passage, 1 Kings 19:14, must, of course, be explained on the same principle. It is not necessary to think of the altars referred to as connected with those at Dan and Bethel. And, though their existence was not in strict accordance with the letter of the law, it had become a temporary necessity. The attitude of the prophets in Israel towards the existing national cultus is manifest in the fact of their forming schools at the famous seats of idolatry, Bethel, (Jericho,) Gilgal, in standing protest against it.

Before we turn to the prophetical books themselves, one point calls for a fuller discussion. The origin and character of the Bamoth-worship (that on high-places) in the kingdom of Judah are of paramount importance for the question of the existence or non-existence of the Codes. It has a bearing on the whole debate concerning the primitive religious state of Israel. The critics claim, that, before the temple at Jerusalem existed, all places of worship were equally honored and sacred. In the time of Solomon, not so much a centralization as an elevation took place of the newly built temple to be the sanctuary *par excellence*. But the Bamoth (high-places) existed all along, and their right of existence was not disputed. The war afterwards waged against them was the result of a higher stage of religious life among the prophets, — that great movement which resulted in the production and enforcement of the Deuteronomic Code. The prophets Amos, Hosea, Isaiah, do not yet condemn the Bamoth *per se,* but simply their corrupting influence tending towards idolatry. It was not an abnormal cultus, but a primitive state of affairs: in one continuous line it can be traced back, from the eighth century upwards, through the reigns of Solomon, David, Saul, into the period of the Judges.

We must begin with denying the last proposition, which is indeed the basis of the whole argument. The statement needs considerable qualification before it will satisfy the facts. These are, that, when there was no legal central sanctuary, the Bamoth-worship was temporarily tolerated, in order that the spontaneous impulse of the pious might find opportunity to express itself. This was the state of affairs from Samuel onward, until the building of Solomon's temple. It was, however, condemned, and considered illegal, as long and as often as the presence of God in his dwelling-place constituted this the only place of worship, as during the period of Judges at Shiloh, and after Solomon's time at Jerusalem. The chain which the critics have fabricated lacks two necessary links: 1. Judges contains no evidence that the worship on high-places was allowed or practiced by the pious. 2. The same evidence is wanting for the time subsequent to the building of the temple in Solomon's reign, till the first only partially successful attempt of Hezekiah to do away with the Bamoth.

The second ground on which this theory rests, is that the earlier prophets do not condemn the worship as sinful *per se,* but only on account of its corrupting tendency. If there are passages in Amos and Hosea which would bear out this meaning, the natural inference is, that they accommodated their teaching to the difficult situation in which the northern people had been placed by the tyranny of their rulers. On the whole, it is very artificial to ascribe such a distinction between "*per se*" and "*per accidens*" to the prophets. Even the law did not prohibit plurality of sanctuaries because of any inherent necessity in the character of Jahveism, but for the practical purpose of securing by unity purity, by centralization elevation of the cultus. When the prophets, in accordance with their general method, do not state the law *in abstracto,* but in its inner meaning; when they emphasize more the final cause of the command than the command itself, — this exhibits only the more strikingly their true relation to the law as its spiritual interpreters. They immediately go to the root of the matter, and state not only the "what," but the "why" also. This is all that the critical distinction amounts to.

The critics themselves must admit that the writer of Kings represents all Bamoth-worship since the building of the temple as unlawful, and imputes it even to the pious kings of Judah as sin, that they did not terminate it. That the latter did not take their stand as strongly against this cultus as afterwards Hezekiah and Josiah, finds its full explanation in what has been remarked. Bamoth-worship, tolerated from Samuel till Solomon, had become a second nature to the people. The consciousness of its abnormal character had been lost. It may have been revived in the pious kings more or less: the people as a whole were not awake to it. The objection, that if such ignorance prevailed, the prophets could not have reckoned neglect of the law as sin, finds its answer in Hos. 4:6. "My people are destroyed for lack of knowledge: because thou hast rejected knowledge, I will also reject thee, that thou shalt be no priest to me: seeing thou hast forgotten the law of thy God." It is as if the passage were written in direct refutation of the critics. To produce a reform among the people, a renewed enforcement by a special divine providence of the prophetical Deuteronomic Code was required, to which point we shall hereafter direct our attention.

Chapter Eighteen - Testimony of the Early Prophets

It will not be necessary for our purpose, to investigate all the amount of evidence that might be collected from the prophetical writings of the Old Testament. We are chiefly concerned with the books of Amos, Hosea, Isaiah, and Micah. Of Joel we cannot make any use, since a number of critics remand his prophecy to the post-exilic period. Jeremiah and Ezekiel wrote after the pretended origin of the Deuteronomic Code. Deutero-Isaiah is declared to be exilic.

The testimony of the earlier prophets has a double weight, since they speak as contemporary witnesses. When the author of the Book of Kings makes mention of the Mosaic laws, the critics are ready to call it one of his anachronisms. This is precluded here. We have no reason to fear that we shall find ourselves hunting our own shadow.

We have first the passages in which a direct reference to the תּוֹרַת יְהֹוָה (*law of Jehovah*) is found. They are in succession the following Amos 2:4; Hos. 4:6, 8:1, 12; Isa. 1:10, 2:3, 5:24, 8:16, 20, 24:5, 30:9; Mic. 4:2.

The value of this testimony seems to be somewhat lessened by the consideration that the phrase " תּוֹרַת יְהֹוָה, תּוֹרָה, absolutely may designate something else than the Mosaic law. On the one hand, the etymology (from יָרָה *jacĕre, ejicĕre, manum extendĕre,* and then *instruĕre, docēre*), on the other hand, the exegesis of some passages, as Isa. 8:16, 30:9; Mic. 4:2, which require the more general sense, go to prove that the phrase may denote *all instruction of God,* whether given in his law, or by the prophets. Compare the instances where תּוֹרָה is parallel with יָרָה (*word*). The Mosaic law doubtless was Thora from the beginning; but that it was Thora in the later specific, traditional sense cannot be proved. All that can be said, is that it was probably the Thora of Jehovah *par excellence.*

We may concede all this without depriving ourselves of the ability to show that the prophets refer and appeal to Mosaic laws. For after the subtraction of all the passages where the general meaning is admissible, we keep a *residuum* where no other sense than that of "*written law*" will satisfy the context.

There are cases where Thora designates God's instructions in days gone by. To this class belong, —

Isa. 24:5: "They have transgressed the laws, changed the ordinance, broken the everlasting Covenant." Thora is here parallel with the "everlasting Covenant," and with "ordinance," the former of which would certainly not apply to "prophetical teaching."

Amos 2:4: "Because they have despised the law of the LORD, and have not kept his commandments, and their lies caused them to err, after the which their fathers have walked."

Hos. 4:6. Here a priestly law had not only been disobeyed, but forgotten, which implies its existence for considerable time. Its knowledge and interpretation are represented as a priestly inheritance.

Hos. 8:1: "Because they have transgressed my Covenant, and trespassed against my law." Here "law" and "Covenant" are synonymous, as in Isa. 24:5.

But the critics will say, How can we know, when Amos, Hosea, and Isaiah refer to a Thora, different from their own words, that this must be the Thora of Moses? Why can it not refer to the teaching of the older prophets, who had preceded those of the ninth and eighth century? We might just as well retort the answer, Why can it not refer to Moses, for he certainly was a prophet? Still, this is not enough. Our claim is, that Moses occupies a unique position. He is the prophet *par excellence,* the legislator to whose work the later prophets appealed, in whose institutions they lived and moved and had their being. We must show, that, in the passages referred to, nothing but the Mosaic law can reasonably be meant. This follows from several considerations: —

1. In two of them the law is used parallel with "Covenant," meaning the conditions which the Covenant imposes. This conception must date back to a definite, historical event, which is, according to the whole Old Testament, the Sinaitic legislation. Hence the Thora which stands parallel to the Covenant must be the Sinaitic Thora.

2. The prophetic word was a fleeting one, which had as yet no permanence and stability. It was God's intention, that it should be preserved for future generations; but till a relatively late period, it served only the needs of the present. It is therefore improbable that Amos, Hosea, and Isaiah should have referred their contemporaries to the words of earlier prophets, who had long ceased to speak, and of the preservation of whose commands there is no evidence. The prophecies in their time were "testimony" in the strictest sense. They came and went, but constituted no codified law.

3. To fall back upon earlier prophets transfers, but does not relieve, the difficulty. So far as we know, the mission of all prophets was to enforce and vindicate the law. They never pretend to introduce a new religion, never require of the people that it shall commit itself to unreasonable authority. All their appeals are addressed to the conscience, the moral or national consciousness of Israel, both of which presuppose the law as their root and norm. Even Smend says, "Antiquitus tradita atque accepta esse oportebat, ad quae prophetae provocare poterant." Now, it will certainly do to say that the younger prophets appealed to the older ones, the later to the earlier. But to what did the older and the earlier appeal? Did *they* stand on their own authority? Did *they* prescribe law, instead of upholding it? To this assertion the critics must resort, but it is out of all analogy. We touch here again the weak spot in the reconstructive scheme. Prophetism, at least incipient prophetism, hangs in the air. It had no seed to spring from, no soil to root in: its origin and growth are involved in a profound mystery. The early prophets, we claim, must have stood on the platform constructed by Moses.

Next comes the passage Hos. 8:12, which deserves to occupy a place by itself, —

אֶכְתָּוב לֹו רֻבֹּו תֹּורָתִי כְּמֹו־זָר נֶחְשָׁבוּ.

We follow the reading of the Kethib, and translate רִבֹּו "ten thousand." Our first remark is, that רִבֹּו תֹּורָתִי can by no means refer to prophetic teaching. It does not matter whether we take רִבֹּו in apposition, or as the *nomen regens* of תֹּורָתִי: in either case, the reference must be to law proper. The prophetic Thora constituted one whole: it appears as synonymous with

114

" דִּבֵּר, a mere abstraction. Accordingly, neither translation— "My Thora, ten thousand," or "Ten thousand of my Thora" — will apply to it. Also the word אֶכְתָּוב precludes all other meanings than that of written law. The prophets, as remarked above, did not teach their contemporaries by writing, but by the living word.

We may infer that the idea of a written law was very familiar in Hosea's time. Whether this verse contains a definite allusion to law actually written, will depend partly on the context, partly on the construction of אֶכְתָּוב.

Keil takes the latter as an historical present, from which the meaning would result, "I have written ten thousand precepts of my law [in the time of Moses], which still exist." But there is no evidence that the Hebrew future ever has such a sense. It is not equivalent to the Greek perfect, but to the Latin imperfect, and denotes repeated action; so that the meaning would be, that God by Moses, and afterwards by the prophets, had repeatedly prescribed law to Israel.

This is, indeed, Ewald's interpretation. There is no evidence, however, of such a legal literature as Ewald imagines to have existed.

We may explain the future with Hitzig as purely hypothetical: "Though I had written ten thousand," etc. But how could the multitude of commandments increase the guilt of disobedience? We would expect that in this case, the prophet had taken as small a number as possible to express this idea.

Smend does not understand the רֻבֵּי of numerous commands, but rather in a qualitative sense, commands minutely stated. This certainly yields a meaning appropriate to the context, but is less suitable to the hypothetical interpretation.

Two more views are possible. Either we may take the future as a *praesens historicum*, not in Keil's sense of the Greek perfect, but in the sense of a simple Hebrew perfect, for which, in the alacrity of discourse, it is often substituted (Gesenius, § 127, 4 c.), or we can understand the future to introduce a conditional clause, —"Even when I write to him ten thousand of my law, they are counted as nothing."

We must choose between the last two constructions, either of which presupposes the existence of a written divine law in the days of Hosea.

The context furnishes no sufficient data to determine what the contents of this law were. Only ver. 11 might give us a glimpse. "Because Ephraim has made many altars to sin, his altars shall be unto him to sin." Ewald considers the two members of the verse as expressing the same thought, which would be nothing more than a truism. The sin which the Israelites had committed consciously in erecting the many altars, cannot be the sin to which God's righteous judgment gave them up. It must have been a new phase of evil consequent upon the former. The most natural explanation is, that because Israel sinned in transgressing the command, which required unity of worship, the many altars would be productive of the further sin of apostasy and idolatry. One sin was punished by a process, a sliding scale of sin. With this interpretation and the immediately following statement of ver. 12, "that God's commands were counted for nothing," we can hardly fail to recognize in it an allusion to the Deuteronomic Code, whose principal aim was to enforce unity of the sanctuary.

Smend, in his "Moses apud Prophetas," admits all this in principle, and still refuses to see in it a proof of the existence of the Pentateuchal Codes. He says (p. 13), "Itaque Hoseae verba octavo saeculo, apud Ephraimitas multas leges scriptas fuisse comprobant...quamvis a magna populi parte negligerentur...ut adeo divini juris videantur, acsi ab ipso Jehova scriptae essent." Page 19, "Certe plurimas illas leges quarum Hosea mentionem facit, ad Mosem inventorem relatas esse putandum est." His argument for this is quite conclusive. All laws, according to the prophets, have their foundation in the Covenant between God and the people. But the Covenant was Sinaitic: "Re vera semel in Monte Sinai per Mosem junctum esse, traditione certissima atque unanimi antiquitas constabat. Ni [Moses] fuisset, prophetarum munus ne cogitari quidem potuisset."

These remarkable confessions give all that can be reasonably demanded. There were many written laws, which the prophet and his contemporaries ascribed to Moses. They were universally neglected. Though their contents cannot be accurately determined, nothing contradictory to the Pentateuchal Codes is ever approved of. The Sinaitic legislation was considered as an historical fact. And, after having granted all this, the critic stands up in his own authority, and declares, "At libros illos, si quidem multi erant non ex antiquissimis temporibus Mosis originem traxisse *jure* concludas!" We ask with what right? Does critical skepticism go so far as to deny the credibility of the prophets' testimony for the time that lay behind them? When Hosea says that God gave the law at Sinai through Moses, shall the critics say, It cannot have been, laws must have gradually appeared? Or, do they desire that Hosea and Amos shall tell us in so many words, "The laws which we refer to are no other than the Mosaic Codes"? There is no evidence that any collection of laws ever existed but the Mosaic. And we must deny to the critics the right of substituting an imaginary one, to do away with the plain meaning of Hosea's words.

As in the historical books, we do not believe that much can here be made of the ceremonial usages and religious customs referred to by the prophets. When we would array it as evidence of the existence of the Codes, Wellhausen would from his standpoint have the right to remind us, "Legem non habentes natura faciunt legis opera." Once more our attitude must be an apologetic one. We must show that the Codes may have existed. [1]

First of all, the critics discover in these prophets an antagonism against the priesthood and ceremonial institutions in general, and consider them as defenders of a more spiritual type of religion. The principal passages are: Amos 5:21, *seqq.*, 8:10; Isa. 1:11, *seqq.*, 29:13; Mic. 6:6-8; Hos. 4:6, 7:14, 10:12, 12:6. Dr. Kuenen says, "The prophets nowhere insist upon fidelity in observing the holy ceremonies. On the contrary, they speak of them with an indifference which borders upon disapproval, sometimes even with unfeigned aversion."

It must be remembered, that Hosea and Amos prophesied in the Northern kingdom, where there was no legal Aaronic priesthood. The priests opposed by the prophets were no rightful priests. Still, they are hardly ever condemned in this official capacity, but for lack of knowledge, for being murderers, robbers, etc. The point at issue is, whether the prophets condemned the ceremonies *per se,* or on account of their wrong performance. An unprejudiced examination of the evidence will not leave us in doubt on which side the truth lies. We note the following points of decisive importance: —

1. If the ceremonies had been condemned by the prophets *per se*, in contrast with a more spiritual religion, Jehovah's attitude ought to have been represented as one of indifference towards them. This is not the case. When Kuenen speaks of "indifference bordering upon disapproval, sometimes unfeigned aversion," all these words are not synonymous indeed, they are mutually exclusive. God disapproves of the ceremonies, not for formal, but for material, reasons. He hates, despises, the feast-days. He will not smell in their solemn assemblies: his ears revolt against the melody of their viols. The ritual is represented as offensive in the highest degree. We are warranted to draw from such positive terms two conclusions: (1) There must have been a positive element of sin in the ritual performances which the prophets condemn. (2) The very fact, that they offend God, awake his hatred and revolt, shows that he stands in a sort of necessary relation towards them. He cannot disregard or abolish the ceremonies, but is obliged (*sit venia verbo*) to attend, to see, to hear. No stronger evidence could be furnished that the ritual was a divine institution, and recognized as such by the prophets. Isa. 1:14 is very instructive in this respect: "They are a *trouble* unto me; I am *weary* to *bear* them."

2. Ceremonies and true piety were so closely allied in the religious consciousness of the time, that even evil-doers thought they could either conciliate by them the favor of God, or at least secure the esteem of the pious. That the right conception of sacrifices was known and shared by the prophets, is not disproved by this self-righteous abuse of the wicked, but on the contrary presupposed by it.

3. The high esteem in which the prophets held the ceremonial, and how far the idea of emancipating Israel from it was outside of their intentions, are shown incidentally several times. In Amos 7:17, the Lord threatens Amaziah "that he shall die in a polluted land." There is a climax in the verse of all evils which would befall the priest, this dying in a polluted land would be the most formidable one. The land and the priest are called pure, not on account of their piety, but on account of the outward worship and cultus of the true Jehovah, which was lacking in heathen lands. Now, if this ritual, as it was represented in a wicked priest, was still sufficiently sacred to make the land of Israel pure, we surely are not warranted to consider Jehovah and his proph-

ets as despisers of the ceremonies. The soil itself contracted purity and impurity from the worship of its inhabitants. Smend calls this sentiment "Levitismus." Of the same character is the passage Hos. 9:1-6 "They shall eat unclean things in Assyria: ...their sacrifices shall be unto them as the bread of mourners; all that eat thereof shall be polluted," etc. (compare also 3:4). Smend confesses, "(Qui) talia judicent iis quae in ipso Levitico inveniuntur nihil cedunt."

4. The passage Isa. 29:13, which has been claimed in favor of the critical view, teaches, properly interpreted, exactly the opposite. The contrast is not between commands given by man and commands prescribed by God, but between those learned from man and those learned from God. The former represents mere external ritualism; the latter inward piety, expressing itself in outward forms. The ceremonial worship of the people was not a spontaneous manifestation of spiritual-mindedness, but worthless compliance with a form from self-righteous motives. This externalism is strikingly characterized as "doing precepts learned from men." Of course, nothing as to the origin of these precepts is decided thereby.

5. The estimate put by the prophets on the ritual system is throughout very favorable. Isaiah associates it with the vision of his great commission (chap. 6). He sees an altar (ver. 6), and smoke (of sacrifices?) (ver. 4). The Egyptians, when converted, will erect an altar and a *mazzebah* (pillar) for a monumental purpose, do sacrifice and oblation, vow a vow, and perform it (chap. 19:19, *seqq.*). Jehovah has a fire in Zion and a furnace in Jerusalem (31:9). In Hos. 4:4 it is counted the highest contumacy to strive with a priest.

6. The passage Amos 5:25, 26, seems to deserve a closer examination. We do not intend to inquire into the kind of idolatry of which the verse speaks, but simply raise the question, whether Amos denies in this passage the antiquity of the ritual in general, or at least of the ritual as it was in his day.

The verse has been interpreted in the most various ways. The question of paramount importance is, whether a positive or negative answer was expected by the prophet. That he supposed the answer to be obvious, is clear; so much so, that he did not even think it necessary to add it.

Vaihinger and Kuenen claim that an affirmative answer is presupposed. Kuenen gives as the meaning, that the Israelites had combined the offering of sacrifices to God with idolatry, and that the prophet takes this as proof of the worthlessness of sacrifices, which were consistent with the greatest apostasy. To this interpretation, there are the following objections: (*a*) The use of הֲ, and not הֲלֹא, leads us to expect a negative answer. Though הֲ may be followed by an affirmation, it is only where the answer is doubtful, never where it is considered as self-evident. (*b*) If the co-existence of Jehovah-worship and idolatry were emphasized, we would expect in ver. 26 a ו *consecut cum futuro;* but there is a perfect וּנְשָׂאתֶם. (*c*) The argument would have been very inconclusive to the contemporaries of the prophet. That the sacrifices of their idolatrous ancestors were worthless, proved nothing against theirs. And if those who are addressed here were idolaters themselves, the prophet would not have used such a far-fetched argument.

The majority of commentators admit that the words imply that the Israelites did not sacrifice to Jehovah in the desert. But they differ widely as to the reason assigned for this: —

(a) It is most commonly held, that the suspension of sacrificial worship was a result of the idolatry described in ver. 26, whatever that may have been. So Keil and Hitzig and many others. Against this interpretation, the following objections are urged: 1. The order of the words in the Hebrew. It is claimed, if Jehovah were contrasted with strange gods, the question would have been introduced by לִי הַ, with the emphasis on *me*. 2. The example of the forty years' wandering in the desert was, according to Keil, intended to show how, from the beginning, the Israelites were a perverse and apostate people. But how can, in ver. 21-24, the excess of ceremonial, and in ver. 25, the suspension of the same, be urged alike as a proof of Israel's iniquity?

(b) The same objection bears against the view of those who separate ver. 25 from the preceding verses. They understand that the prophet addresses in this verse other persons than in ver. 21-24. After having rebuked those who self-righteously put their trust in sacrifices, he now proceeds to condemn the false security of others based on the Covenant of Sinai by reminding them that the Covenant had already been broken in the desert. But there is no trace in the context of a transition from the persons first addressed to others.

(c) Smend's interpretation is, that the prophet wishes to show that God's favor was not dependent on outward ceremonies, and that for this purpose he refers to the sojourn in the wilderness, during which, notwithstanding the fact that the ritual was necessarily suspended, still God's favor was not withdrawn. Of course, this makes it necessary to understand ver. 26 either of the present or of the future. Smend translates with Ewald: "Ergo tolletis; i.e., cum idolis vestris exsulatum abibitis." To this view it may be objected, 1. We would, if the subjects of ver. 25 and 26 were not the same, expect to see the latter introduced by וְעַתָּה, or something analogous. 2. It is doubtful whether the preterite can be used in this connection in the future sense, which Smend ascribes to it. We may add, however, that it is necessary to take the verb in ver. 27 as a future, and why not, then, ver. 26 also? 3. The forty years' wandering in the desert are always considered elsewhere as a period of apostasy, in which God's favor was actually withdrawn. The only consideration in favor of this view lies in the separation of ver. 25 from the verses 21-23 by ver. 24. The latter verse seems to begin the statement of what God did require in contrast with what he did not demand in ver. 21-23. We might infer from this, that the conduct of the Israelites in the desert is referred to as an exponent of what was really well-pleasing to God.

We do not pretend to give a new and better explanation of this difficult passage than any one stated above. But we have certainly shown that nothing can be inferred from it inconsistent with the high antiquity of the Sinaitic legislation. We may once more quote Smend, who says with regard to it, "Attamen falluntur qui quum certas Pentateuchi leges recentiores esse contendunt se Amoso teste uti putant."

[1] On this point, compare what was said on a previous page in regard to the historical books.

Chapter Nineteen - Testimony of the Poetical Books

Delitzsch assures us that the literature of the time of David and Solomon presupposes the existence of the entire Thora in its present form. He verifies this statement by several quotations, of which the greater part do doubtless show acquaintance with the Pentateuch. Still, we would be greatly mistaken if we considered his argument as decisive. What Delitzsch assigns to the Davidic and Solomonic age, becomes with our present critics the product of a much later time. Reuss supposes Job to have been written about the time of the destruction of the Northern kingdom, before Deuteronomy and the Priest Code were as yet in existence; and that the Song of Solomon was composed shortly after the schism. He declares that his doubts do not go so far as to deny to the period of the Kings the composition of any Psalm whatever. After this magnanimous and liberal concession, he hastens to add that it must be limited to the first division of the Psalter, which originally contained Ps. 3-41. Even the largest part of this is post-Deuteronomic, the whole collection not pre-exilic; and for our present purpose we would retain nothing more than Ps. 2, 18, 20, 21 (45, 46, 49). Probably the Psalter contains no Davidic Psalms at all.

He claims that the Solomonic authorship of not a single line in the Book of Proverbs can be proved. The book, as a whole, was published after the exile. Koheleth (Ecclesiastes) is remanded to the time of the Ptolemies, 200 B.C.

Reuss, however, goes farther, especially with regard to the Psalms, than the very boldest among German doubters have done. Hitzig and Ewald agree on the Davidic origin of at least Ps. 3, 4, 7, 8, 11, 19a. Ewald admits in addition, 2, 20, 21, 24, 29, 32, 110. Hitzig, on the other hand, 9, 10, 12, 13, 15, 16, 17, 19b. Leaving out of the account those Psalms which both Hitzig and Ewald consider as pre-Deuteronomic, we obtain the number of twenty-one Psalms, to which we may safely appeal, without being suspected of traditional prejudice in calling our witnesses.

After all this deduction, our harvest must be scanty. Its power lies, not so much in the number of witnesses as in the unequivocal character of their testimony. A single indisputable mention of the Thora, or reference to it, outweighs many arguments *e silentio*. The former leaves no choice: the latter do.

A most important objection to the newer theory of religious development may be drawn from the deep spiritual conceptions, the lofty moral sentiments, which these Davidic Psalms breathe throughout. A David who was the prototype of the picture drawn by the critics could not have written such hymns. He could by no means have anticipated what lay hidden in the future consciousness of prophetism two centuries after his reign. All the laws of development protest against it. Moreover, there is no trace in his songs of that peculiar reaction against an exaggerated ritual which characterizes the prophets of the ninth and the eighth centuries. The outward is here the clear mirror in which the inward throws its spontaneous reflex. This leads to a twofold observation: 1. When spiritual religion and ceremonial worship conflicted afterwards, this cannot have been the original, normal relation, but must be considered as the result of externalization of the ritual. Thus, the testimony of the prophets, that Israel's religious state was one of apostasy, is verified anew. 2. This spiritual conception of the law as we find it in David cannot be the product of a natural development, but testifies to a divine origin of both the spirit and the letter. Whether a development of religion by contrasts on the principle of negativity may, or may not, account for the opposition to ceremonies on the part of the prophets, it certainly fails to explain the synthesis of this spiritual appreciation in David. The following passages are noteworthy in this respect Ps. 4:5, *seqq.*, 7:8, 9, *seqq.*, 15, passim, 20:3, *seqq.*, 24:3, 4, and especially the whole of 32.

The "judgments" of the LORD are mentioned (10:5); his words (12:6), "his judgments and statutes (18:22). The second part of the nineteenth Psalm speaks of the Thora in a way not different from that in which a Jew after the exile would have done. It is easy to remand all this to Maccabean times; but when even Hitzig concedes the Davidic origin, we may safely say that our critics have no other reason to deny it than an over-anxious regard for their own hypothesis.

Zion is the only legal sanctuary, where God dwells in the center of his people (9:11); the holy temple, a symbol of his heavenly dwelling-place (11:4); the tabernacle, to which only the pure and righteous may ideally approach (15:1, *seqq.*), from whence help is sent in the day of trouble (20:1, 2); his holy place (24:3), from whence the rod of his strength is sent (110:2), where the cherubs are attached to the ark as a symbol of his throne and power (18:10).

It may also be remarked, that in Ps. 7:7 the term עֵדָה occurs, which, according to Wellhausen, can only be understood in connection with the Levitical system, and is therefore post-exilic. The few instances that it occurs in Judges may be set to the account of a redactor, but in a Davidic Psalm this will not do. Perhaps also 110:4 implies a contrast with the Aaronic priesthood.

Ps. 24:4 reminds us of the third commandment in a very striking way. Ps. 4 has several allusions to the very words of the Covenant-law; likewise Ps. 16 (Compare Delitzsch in Luth. Zeitschrift, 1882, Heft vi.).

Neither do references to the historical portions of the Pentateuch fail. Ps. 7:6, קוּמָה, "arise," and verse 7, שׁוּרָה, "return," may be compared with Num.

121

10:35,36 (Jehovistic); 17:8, אִישׁוֹן בַּת עֵין, with Deut. 23:10, אִישׁוֹן עֵינוֹ;Ps. 11:6, אֵשׁ וְגָפְרִית, with Gen. 19:24.

Some of the allusions which Delitzsch finds in Proverbs are of no use for our purpose. The "tree and the way of life" are both Jehovistic; so that, when the critics assign a relatively late date to the collection of Proverbs, they lose their value. The comparison of Deut. 6:6, 8, with Prov. 7:3; Lev. 19:36 with Prov. 11:1, has more force.

A connection between Canticles 6:13 and Gen. 32:1, 2, cannot be proved. Neither is it necessary to translate Job 31:33 "as Adam." But the allusions in Job 31:11 to Lev. 18:17; of ver. 8-12 to Deut. 22:22; of ver. 26-28 to Deut. 17:2-5, can hardly be denied. Even Kuenen calls them far from improbable. And, as we saw, even Reuss thinks that Job is pre-Deuteronomic.

Chapter Twenty - Second Kings 22 & Nehemiah 8-10

We conclude our survey with a short discussion of the critical view of the narrative found in these chapters. After all that has been said, we may approach them without any prepossession, and consider them as mere historical records, which have to be interpreted in their own light.

Our criticism of the *pia fraus* theory imposed on 2 Kings 22 is the following: —

1. According to the critics, the forgery of the Deuteronomic Code was a skillful stroke of policy, to which a despondent reform-party resorted as the only means of reaching its ends. It had failed in the days of Hezekiah, and its failure was a defeat. The terms in which Kuenen speaks of the situation, imply that the party-lines must have been sharply drawn. There was an opposition to the centralizing Mosaic tendency; and it was strong, influential, and fully on its guard against every movement of the latter. Notwithstanding this, the bare assertion of the reformers, that their program was of Mosaic origin, sufficed to silence all these opponents, many of whom were doubtless reduced to poverty and disgrace, or even exposed to death by the intended reform. No trace of resistance is discovered: all the people stood to the Covenant. We cannot but observe that all this does not resemble the usual execution of a *coup d'état*. For this sudden change in the relation of the parties, Dr. Kuenen gives no other reason than what might be called an appeal to the maxim, *"Cujus regio, illius religio."* The regal power was in the East and in Judah unlimited. The majority of the people complied with the will and command of their princes. How utterly inadequate such general phrases are to explain the pretended situation, will not escape any thoughtful observer of the facts.

2. It is improbable, if the so-called Mosaic party stood in favor with the king, and if the forgery was perpetrated within the very circle aspiring to such favor, and relying upon it for future success, that the author or authors

would have extended their threatenings to the monarch himself in such a way as is here done (Deut. 28:36).

3. If the chief or only ends which the forgers had in view were abolition of idolatry and Bamoth-worship, it is hard to see why they put themselves to the unnecessary trouble of writing a whole Code, containing numerous laws which served no present purpose whatever.

4. It should also be remembered, that the practice of forgery, as it is now claimed by the critics for the origin of Deuteronomy and the Priest Code, stands unparalleled in the whole domain of Old-Testament literature. The Pseudepigraphae are all of later date, and without exception owe their origin to far lower tendencies than we are warranted to ascribe to the Mosaic party of King Josiah's time.

We now turn to Neh. 8-10. The credibility of these chapters was at first doubted by Dr. Kuenen in 1861. Afterwards, in 1870, he retracted these doubts; since his whole hypothesis respecting the origin of the Priest Code was based on the facts which they contain. The two important and decisive questions to be answered here are, —

1. What portion of the Pentateuch did the law read by Ezra comprehend?

2. What inferences may be drawn from Ezra's knowledge and the people's ignorance of this law?

To the first question, critics have but one answer. Unanimously they declared the book of the law to have been the priestly legislation. To prove this, they commonly refer to what is said regarding the feast of tabernacles. We must remark, however, that this is far from settling the point in dispute. That Lev. 23 belonged to the law that was read, by no means shows that the Priest Code alone constituted this law. So far from this being the case, there are several reasons which forbid us to assume it.

1. The reading was continued for at least ten days, and the first day for six hours. The terms seem to imply that this reading was not a mere rehearsal of what had been read before. It is, then, necessary to assume that the law-book was more comprehensive than Leviticus. When we remember that the Deuteronomic Code was read before the king and the people at one time, this conclusion will appear all the more necessary.

2. The reading of the law seems to have been in execution of the command, Deut. 31:11. Though Deuteronomy speaks only of each seventh year, we can easily conceive that the first opportunity to comply with the newly published command was eagerly seized upon. From Neh. 10:31, it appears that hitherto the Year of Jubilee had not been observed. It was therefore necessary to compute the seven years from the publication of the law onward; and thus the current year became, *ipso facto*, a Sabbath-year, which required the reading of the law. We conclude that not only the Priest Code, but also the Deuteronomic law, was read.

3. Evidently the confession made by the Levites on the twenty-fourth day of the month, contained in chap. 9, is in substance and form the echo of the

frequent and diligent study of the newly published law during the three previous weeks. Its contents furnish the best means of identifying the law referred to. Now, a careful examination will convince us that this confession is full of reminiscences, not only of the Elohistic narrative, but just as well of that of the Jehovist and of Deuteronomy.

4. The promises made by the people are characteristic of the Jehovistic and Deuteronomic law. As such we note the promise not to intermarry with strange nations (Neh. 10:30; Exod. 34:16; Deut. 7:3), the promise to intermit the exaction of debts every seventh year (ver. 31; Deut. 15:2), the promise to offer the corn, the new wine, and oil (ver. 37, 39; Deut. 12:17).

All these considerations favor the view, that Ezra did not publish the Priest Code merely, but the whole Mosaic Thora, Elohist and Jehovist and Deuteronomist. The historical credibility of the narrative cannot be doubted. The confession, as reported in chap. 9, must be authentic. In denying it, the critics would destroy the only basis on which they rest their theory of the Ezraic origin of the Priest Code.

Let us now consider the second question. What are we to hold respecting Ezra's relation to the law, which he is said to have read before the people?

It has become almost an axiom with the latest critics, that Ezra was, if not the author, at least the redactor, of the Elohistic legislation. "The law of God was in his hand" (Ezra 7:14) when he went to Jerusalem, in the year 458 B.C. Between this date and the return under Zerubbabel and Joshua, 536 B.C., lies a period of nearly eighty years, concerning whose history, as far as the remaining exiles are concerned, we know absolutely nothing. This utter ignorance has afforded the critics a splendid chance to spin out their famous theory of the gradual origin of the Priest Code. Where history has left no record, conjectural criticism has not only free play, but seems to a certain extent justified and commendable.

The starting-point is Ezekiel's program. Kuenen and others are candid enough to admit that his work is no just exponent of the general sentiment prevailing among the exiles. In his time his figure is unique. So far as Ezekiel's testimony goes, the people of his day were by no means the priestly Israel which the prophet describes in his visionary Thora. We have no ground to assume, that, besides him, others were occupied with the elaboration of a ritualistic system. In his own words (specially chap. 20), his priestly character stands out in bold contrast with the indifference or anti-Jahvistic tendencies of the mass. Even the following generation seems not to have been influenced by his Thora, as no traces of an attempt to execute it appear. We believe that the Book of Ezekiel, as a whole, does not give the impression that the exiles troubled themselves in Babylon with writing priestly law.

Far less can the theory find support in the writings of the pretended Deutero-Isaiah. If he wrote immediately before the capture of Babylon by Cyrus, we have but one explicit testimony the more, that, among the best elements of the captivity, no such priestly tendencies prevailed. Deutero-Isaiah speaks "like one of the old prophets," if not actually, still seemingly opposed to all ritualism. Isa. 58 is decisive in this respect.

Neither does it appear that special stress was laid on the priestly ceremonial side of their religion by the exiles who returned in 536. We need not assume that intentional disobedience prevailed at the beginning, but that soon a lack of zeal manifested itself may be seen from Haggai and Zechariah. How much Ezra and Nehemiah found to reform afterwards, is abundantly known. Surely, if such an attachment to the temple-service and the ceremonial side of the national life had existed among the exiles in Babylon, as could produce a lively interest in the law, even as to its theoretical aspects, we may take for granted that the history of the new colony would have shaped itself differently.

These are positively all the data from which we can obtain any *a priori* information as to the eight decades which, according to many critics at present, enclose the mysterious birth of a whole legal system in their unknown and ever unknowable history. *A posteriori* there is but a single fact which gives us a glimpse into the dark past, - the fact that Ezra came from Babylon, with the law in his hand, as the ready scribe, evidently with the purpose to instruct his countrymen, and revive their zeal for the work of God amongst them.

A correct estimate of these historical data will immediately show whether the view, that during these eighty years the Priest Code was framed, deserves to be put on the list of plausible theories, or under the head of "legal fictions," fanciful and arbitrary alike.

Notwithstanding our utter lack of historical information, Kuenen, Wellhausen, and Reuss undertake to tell us how within its limits the priestly laws successively made their appearance. There was first the so-called "Law of Holiness," comprising Lev. 17-26. Next comes a group consisting of Exod. 12, 25-31, Lev. 1-17, 24, 27, and most of the priestly portions in Numbers. From both is still distinguished a third group containing later additions.

1. To this whole scheme we must, first of all, object the lack of all positive evidence, that the work of codifying ritual law was carried on in Babylon on such a grand scale. Where do the least traces appear in Ezekiel, Deutero-Isaiah, Haggai, Zechariah, the Book of Ezra, and of Nehemiah, we do not say of the completion of the process (for this simply begs the whole question), but of the tendencies that originated or the influences that favored and ripened it?

But more than this. If we realize the situation well, we cannot but doubt the critics' assumption, that in the circles that remained at Babylon when the first colony set out for Jerusalem, there was enough of productive energy to create all at once what centuries had not been able to produce when the nation was still prosperous and independent, and the temple-service flourishing and in high esteem.

First of all, the better element must have joined Zerubbabel and Joshua. Those who remained were certainly the least influenced by theocratic concern in the restoration of the temple-worship and the repossession of the holy city. Ezra 1:5 states that those whose spirit God had raised, went up to build the house of the Lord. The rest seem to have been on the whole indifferent, and to have preferred the riches of Babylon to the wants and dangers of the little caravan that set its face towards Jerusalem.

Secondly, the majority of the priesthood returned, and comparatively a small number of priests remained in Babylon. The priests were least of all likely to prefer captivity in a polluted land to a relative freedom in the holy city. And what adds a decisive weight to this, is the fact that not less than four thousand priests joined the expedition of Zerubbabel; and with Ezra there went only two priestly families, which cannot have been very numerous (Ezra 8:2).

We have the indisputable facts that the theocratic element left Babylon, and that amongst the worldly remnant, there was only a comparatively small number of priests, and these so indifferent to the land and people of God, that only two of their families were induced to return under Ezra's protection.

Now, the critics wish us to believe two facts which strangely contrast with the two we have just stated: 1. That among the better element, which rebuilt Jerusalem and the temple, and restored its service, there was a development for the worse in an anti-theocratic direction. 2. That among the remnant in Babylon, who had no temple amongst them, and evidently no intentions of ever returning, there was such an interest awakened in the temple-service, that a long literary activity ensued, which resulted in the production of a complete elaborated Code, called by the modern critics the Priest Code.

This demand upon our credulity is most unreasonable. The view contradicts all historic probability. That it is so boldly and persistently maintained, is due to the fact, that, where historical records fail, critical ingenuity is at liberty to fill up the blank with any picture of the imagination whatever.

Dr. Kuenen has felt this difficulty very seriously. He tries to remove it in his own peculiar way, by a number of considerations, which would have force to convince us if we could grant the premises on which they rest. That the Jews were eagerly looking for a future, more favorable, occasion to return, we will have to believe when it is proved. Why had they not joined the expedition which departed under such auspicious circumstances, with the favor and protection of Cyrus, in direct fulfillment of ancient prophecies, those of Jeremiah at least, to leave Deutero-Isaiah out of view? That they were desirous of religious instruction, may be admitted in a general sense; but their attitude does not exhibit interest in that aspect of the Jewish religion which was inseparable from the sanctuary. When afterwards men like Ezra and Nehemiah arose amongst them, their character was not the fruit of the natural state of affairs, but rather a new factor introduced by a special divine intervention to provide for a special need of God's people. The inferences which Kuenen draws from Zech. 6:9-15 are entirely too sweeping. That a few men had come from Babylon, whose arrival is evidently stated as an exceptional case, cannot be made to prove that the great body of the exiles entertained a lively interest in what happened at Jerusalem.

The main objection against the whole scheme lies in its impracticability. Here, as in the case of Deuteronomy, the question recurs, What made it necessary for Ezra to ascribe his laws to Moses? What accounts for the element of fraud entering this piece of Jewish legislation also, as we are asked to believe?

Critics answer, when Ezra arrived at Jerusalem, he found the colonists far below his ideal of righteous Israelites. After a first successful attempt at reform, Ezra is silent for thirteen years. The reasons for this interruption were chiefly twofold. 1. He saw the necessity of adapting his law, formed in Babylon, to the circumstances of the people. 2. He must have met already in his first reform, as well as afterwards, with a strong and influential opposition, as appears from Neh. 13 and Malachi's prophecy. It was in part the zelotic spirit, which both Ezra and Nehemiah manifested, partly more material objections against their innovations, which led to this resistance. The reform involved a limitation of liberty, imposed heavy duties upon the laymen, and on the whole showed a decidedly hierarchical tendency. On the other hand, it bound the priests themselves henceforward to a written word, and thus essentially modified their position. Such a radical revolution did not fail to cause a strong reaction, both from among the people and the priesthood. Hence the claim of Mosaic origin for the Code was absolutely necessary to the success of Ezra's plans.

So we meet here again with the same remarkable phenomena as in the case of Deuteronomy. There it was "the people stood to the Covenant." Here they make a sure covenant, write it, and seal unto it (Neh. 9:38). And in both cases alike the opposition is silent, no word of resistance is uttered, no murmuring or dissenting voice heard. The question recurs here as there: How was this possible, if Ezra's Thora was a mere fiction? If it was genuine and Mosaic, we can understand why the opponents desisted. But suppose them to have been fully on their guard, to have watched Ezra's every movement, to have kept him in suspense for thirteen years, and then finally to have accepted in the most meek and submissive way the most radical changes, contrary to their own opinions and interests, simply because Ezra pretended that his law was Mosaic!

The story sounds incredible, and still we must believe it if the critics are right. We can the less conceive that the opponents were misled on this occasion by the appearances, since, as we have seen, the Priest Code was already combined with the Jehovistic and Deuteronomic laws, and was read together with them. What appears as an addition, and in so far modifies the old, is, *per se,* exposed to suspicion. Still, Ezra's Code was not suspected: the people made a sure covenant, and sealed unto it.

It would certainly seem safer, in view of all these impossibilities, to adhere to the old notion, be it traditional or not, that Ezra published the Thora in no other capacity than that of a ready scribe, who had prepared his heart to seek the law of the Lord, and to do it, and to teach in Israel statutes and judgments; that he did this at a special occasion of the feast of trumpets, at a special request of the people, who expressed by this desire their gratitude for the final completion of the walls of Jerusalem under the supervision of Nehemiah.

Chapter Twenty-One - Did Moses Write The Laws?

We have hitherto occupied ourselves exclusively with the question whether the claim of Mosaic origin which the Codes make for themselves could be vindicated. A few remarks may be added now with regard to the related question whether Moses committed the laws to writing.

That only the Book of the Covenant and the Deuteronomic Code are expressly stated to have been written by Moses, was remarked on a previous page. It will be necessary to keep in mind what was argued there, that these emphatic statements with reference to a part can never disprove the view that Moses wrote the whole.

On the other hand, if it could be shown that Moses wrote only these parts of the legislation, this would not contradict the statements of the Pentateuch itself. Caution is more than anywhere else required on this point of the discussion. The fact is remarkable, that all parts of the Pentateuch, of which it is expressly said that *Moses wrote them,* are Jehovistic-Deuteronomic, have one common style, arid are of the same prophetic character. Even if the critics could settle it beyond doubt that the writer of the Priest Code was not the same with the author of the Book of the Covenant and of Deuteronomy, still the statements of the Pentateuch concerning its own origin would stand untouched.

Doubts have repeatedly been expressed whether the art of writing was known among the Semitic peoples, and among the Israelites in particular, during the Mosaic age (compare Reuss, Geschichte des A. T., § 76). In general, however, the possibility, and even probability, of this knowledge at that time are now recognized. Dr. Kuenen says, "That the Israelites possessed an alphabet, and knew the art of writing, in the Mosaic age, is not subject to reasonable doubt, and now almost universally admitted." The objection which he raises against an extensive practice of the arts of reading and writing among the Israelites from their more frequent mention in Deuteronomy than in the middle books, has since then lost all its power, because Dr. Kuenen himself at present assigns the priority to Deuteronomy.

The Greeks received their knowledge of the art of writing from Semitic colonists. But whence did the Semitic tribes obtain this knowledge? Two answers have been given to this question. Until recently, many favored the derivation of the Semitic alphabet from Babylon or the cuneiform inscriptions of Assyria. At present, however, the opinion seems to prevail among Egyptologists, that the alphabet came from Egypt to the Semites, and was transferred by them to the Greeks, and farther West.

Dr. Taylor, a recent writer on this subject, says (I. p. 133), "It is proved beyond controversy (from the Moabite stone), that the Semitic alphabet was fully developed and established as early as the beginning of the ninth century; while, to the practiced eye of the paleographer, it also indicates that alphabetic writing must have been in familiar use for a very considerable precedent period" (compare also Ewald's "History of Israel," I. p. 52, *seqq.*).

On another page (p. 139), Dr. Taylor sums up his conclusion from the facts in this statement: "The external evidence connects in an unmistakable manner the date of the origin of the alphabet with the period of the sojourn of Israel in Egypt."

Reconstructive criticism is ready to combine with the denial of the historical character of the Pentateuch its own hypothetical conception of the primitive state of Israel during the sojourn in Egypt and the journey in the desert. We are reminded over and over again, that the Jews were a wild nomad-tribe possessing only the first germs of civilization. This view, it must be remembered, rests on no historical grounds whatever. According to the Pentateuch, not only was Moses instructed in all the wisdom of Egypt, but also the Israelites, as a whole, became from nomads a settled people being influenced by Egyptian civilization. They dwelt in houses, not by themselves, but among the Egyptians, sustained friendly relations to the latter, and adopted most of their arts. When we consider how easily the Jews have at all times assimilated the elements of foreign civilization, it admits no longer of any doubt, that, at the time of the exodus, they were something entirely different from the nomad-tribes imagined by the critics. There is no ground, accordingly, for making a distinction, as Reuss does, between Moses and the other Israelites, as if the former had been the only cultured person amongst them, and the rest an uncivilized horde.

It makes no difference whether we assume with Ewald and De Rougé that the Semitic alphabet was transmitted from the Hyksos to the Phoenicians, or suppose with Lenormant and Sayce that the reverse took place: the fact is firmly established, that the Hebrews, before their exodus, had an alphabet; and, as Ewald says, "We need not scruple to assume that Israel knew and used it in Egypt before Moses."

That the Egyptian priests were accustomed to write their laws and sanitary prescriptions, is well known. Diodorus says that the physicians belonged to the priestly class, received their salary from the government, and were bound in their treatment of diseases by a written law made up by many of the most famous of old doctors.

Abstractly, it is not impossible to suppose that even such comprehensive laws as the Priest Code contains might have been orally transmitted in priestly circles. Perhaps the hypothesis might account for a gradual development of law consistent with a germinal or substantial Mosaic origin. But in view of the course of Hebrew history with its numerous relapses, as in the days of Eli, Ahab, Ahaz, Manasseh, and at other critical points, the preservation of a traditionary Code would be scarcely less than a miracle. The fate of Deuteronomy suggests what might have become of a law existing only in the mouth of an apostate priesthood.

To this, two other considerations may be added. We have explicit testimony that the Covenant-law was written in a book, and the Decalogue on tables of stone. To assume a codification of the priestly laws is simply to argue from analogy, or rather *a fortiori;* for if the people had their Code, much more the priests, whose lips should keep knowledge, and at whose mouth one should seek the law.

Finally, we learn that in his last days it was Moses' chief concern to write down the Deuteronomic discourses. The end testifies to the whole. We may expect, if he took care to fix the Deuteronomic Code in written form, and thus solemnly bound the people by a permanent allegiance to God, that he at the same time would protect them against oppression on the part of the priesthood, which wielded such extraordinary influence in Egypt. This could be done in no better way than by codifying and publishing the divinely authenticated rule, by which both priesthood and people would be bound in the future.

So far, therefore, as inherent probability goes, we must accept, together with the Mosaic origin of the Pentateuchal Codes, the view that they were written either by Moses, or by others under his direction and superintendence.